REPAIRING
YOUR
CHRISTIAN
MARRIAGE

CONTENTS

Kylah, Trinity,
and Jurnee,

you are my precious angels,
my gifts from God, and my reason.

For general information on our other products and services or to obtain technical support, please contact our Customer Care Department within the United States at (866) 744-2665, or outside the United States at (510) 253-0500.

Rockridge Press publishes its books in a variety of electronic and print formats. Some content that appears in print may not be available in electronic books, and vice versa.

TRADEMARKS: Rockridge Press and the Rockridge Press logo are trademarks or registered trademarks of Callisto Media Inc. and/or its affiliates, in the United States and other countries, and may not be used without written permission. All other trademarks are the property of their respective owners. Rockridge Press is not associated with any product or vendor mentioned in this book.

Interior and Cover Designer: Amanda Kirk
Art Producer: Sara Feinstein
Editor: Lauren O'Neal
Production Editor: Ruth Sakata Corley

Unless otherwise indicated scripture quotations are from THE HOLY BIBLE, NEW INTERNATIONAL VERSION®, NIV® Copyright © 1973, 1978, 2011 by Biblica, Inc.® Used by permission. All rights reserved worldwide.

Scripture quotations marked ESV are from the ESV® Bible (The Holy Bible, English Standard Version®), copyright © 2001 by Crossway Bibles, a publishing ministry of Good News Publishers. Used by permission. All rights reserved.

Scripture quotations marked GNT are from the Good News Translation in Today's English Version- Second Edition Copyright © 1992 by American Bible Society. Used by Permission.

Scripture quotations marked KJV are from the King James Version of the Bible. Public domain.

Scripture quotations marked NKJV are from New King James Version®.
Copyright © 1982 by Thomas Nelson. Used by permission. All rights reserved.

Cover photography © Beatrix Boros/Stocksy. Interior photography © Busà Photography/Getty, p. vi-vii; all other interior photography © Beatrix Boros/Stocksy.

ISBN: Print 978-1-64152-534-3 | eBook 978-1-64152-535-0

R0

REPAIRING YOUR CHRISTIAN MARRIAGE

Faith-Based Strategies to Rebuild Your Relationship

PATRICE WEBB BUSH

ROCKRIDGE
PRESS

INTRODUCTION

*But those who marry will face
many troubles in this life.*

1 Corinthians 7:28

As a Christian woman, I love, worship, and serve God. As a therapist with master's degrees in social work and counseling, I draw from my faith while also using scientifically developed therapeutic modalities to treat and serve clients. I've spent the past 15 years counseling families—not just in my private practice, It Takes 2 Marriage Coaching, but also as a writer, speaker, and radio host. During that time, I've found that there are many advantages to combining the paradigms of faith and scientific perspective—and I'm not alone.

According to *Psychology Today*, research indicates that religious faith "is associated with better mental health." On this point psychologists and pastors seem to agree. One of the most popular services offered in my private practice is facilitating marriage retreats and workshops for churches, and I've found that many pastors acknowledge the positive potential of using faith *and* science to address the obstacles couples face. They want couples not only to know and understand how scripture applies to their life, but also to have concrete strategies to help get them through the many challenges that marriage presents. Serving couples according to those needs is the specialty of my practice. Rooted in scripture and full of tested therapeutic strategies, this book will bring you some of the most effective ideas and activities I've used with others to enhance your own marriage.

It's *hard work* to do the *heart work* of a relationship. We all want a garden full of colorful flowers, but in order to get there we must first dig up the weeds. Those weeds are the problems that have sprouted in your relationship, but with this book, you'll dig them out by the roots and give those beautiful flowers room to bloom. Make sure you have a notebook or journal at the ready, because I encourage you to write down, share, and discuss what resonates with you along the way.

No matter what difficulties you and your spouse are facing, I believe that this book will help you overcome them as you combine faith and practical action to repair and strengthen your marriage.

Therefore shall a man leave his father and his mother, and shall cleave unto his wife: and they shall be one flesh.

Genesis 2:24 (KJV)

CHAPTER ONE

TO LEAVE AND CLEAVE

FROM THE BEGINNING OF TIME, GOD HAS commanded us to be joined together. How can this simple verse from Genesis be so difficult to follow in real life? To successfully "leave and cleave" requires work. This chapter will look at what's preventing you and your spouse from cleaving to each other as one flesh—in a fully cooperative, healthy, and happy partnership—and how you can fix it.

THE PAST

Often, a couple is not exactly sure when their marriage troubles began. Exactly when and how did you and your spouse go from getting butterflies in your stomach whenever you saw each other to fighting all the time? Let's take a moment to look back. What factors from the past might be affecting you and your spouse now? What's preventing you from leaving behind your upbringing or anything else from your past that interferes with your ability to cleave to your spouse?

Where Are You Coming From?

The beginning of love is what I call the "better than chocolate" stage. During this stage, we're getting to know our partners on a deeper level, learning what makes them tick and what makes their hearts smile. You learn all about how your partner loves scary movies, hates to be alone, is terrified of bugs, or enjoys long walks on the beach. You learn family trees and histories. Getting to know your partner is often exhilarating, as there's always excitement in learning something new.

And unbeknownst to you, while you're learning all about your future spouse's history, you're gathering the very information you need to know in order to put social learning theory into practice. According to social learning theory, we can make observations about a person's present-day behaviors and how they stem from what they were socially taught—in their family, at school, in society at large, and so on. This helps us understand how and why our partners do what they do. (It can also help us extend grace to them in certain situations.)

Learning your partner's history is as important to your relationship as learning their name. To understand someone's history is to understand that person in their current situation—to know where they're coming from. That knowledge makes it possible for you to work as a team with your spouse to overcome the issues that both your histories may be contributing to in your marriage.

Take Shannon and Mike, for example. Shannon grew up with a workaholic mother who often made promises but was too busy at work to follow through on them. As a result, Shannon has a hard time trusting that people mean what they say. Mike, on the other hand, came from a family with dependable parents who valued honesty highly. When Shannon and Mike first started dating, Shannon wasn't even sure she wanted to get married at all. She came to love Mike and enjoyed spending time with him, but she didn't trust him to follow through on commitments or keep his promises, because in her experience, that just wasn't how people acted. How could she "cleave" to anyone when she was so used to being let down? As they got to know each other more, Mike began to understand why Shannon had trust issues, and he worked to earn her trust by consistently keeping his word to her. Eventually, Shannon was able to leave behind her pattern of distrust and cleave to Mike in marriage.

LOOKING BACK

Think back to that "better than chocolate" phase of your relationship when you first met. What were your expectations about marriage? How did your history impact those expectations? Write down your thoughts in your journal or notebook.

Did you have conversations about these expectations with your partner early on in your relationship? Can you recall the views on marriage that your partner expressed when you were dating? Were your expectations in alignment? Journal your thoughts.

How and why have your expectations changed over time? Are they still in alignment? Write in your journal one last time, then compare answers.

Relationship Expectations

Sometimes separating from your family of origin, as Genesis advises, is easier said than done. You and your spouse come from certain backgrounds, and those backgrounds will inform how you relate to each other and what kind of habits, beliefs, and expectations you bring into the relationship. If you grew up in a household where your mom did all the cooking and cleaning while your dad worked outside the home, you may expect your marriage to work like that as well—and if your spouse has different expectations, you may find yourselves in conflict.

In my private practice, I see couples who disagree on what some would consider the simple things. They have major arguments about who should do the dishes, who should put the kids to bed, and so on. Have you and your spouse ever experienced these challenges? If so, did you resolve them, or did you sweep them under the rug and continue having the same fight over and over? You may have physically left the household you grew up in, but do you also need to leave behind certain thoughts and beliefs in order to help your marriage flourish?

Part of leaving and cleaving is coming up with expectations and rules that work for your marriage. Not your parents' marriage, not your in-laws' marriage—*yours*. This is true for big issues and small ones. For example, you might have grown up hearing that the man of the family is responsible for the finances. But in your own marriage, the best policy might be to designate the person who is more interested in or better at money management, regardless of gender. You might also schedule a monthly meeting to go over finances together or split up financial tasks between you. What's important is that you cleave to each other rather than to the way you've always been told things should be done.

THE PRESENT

Now that we've taken the opportunity to look back at the roots of your relationship, let's look around us in the present. What is getting in the way of you and your spouse cleaving to each other right now?

Where Does It Hurt?

Let's say you visit your doctor's office because you're experiencing some back pain. Your doctor will ask you questions like "Where does it hurt—in your upper back or your lower back? On the left side or the right side? Does it hurt when you bend over, or when you stand up straight?" The doctor is trying to gauge your pain points.

What do you and your spouse fight about most often? What makes you feel frustrated? These are the pain points in your marriage. Some of the most common are parenting, sex, trust, shared responsibilities, and finances.

IDENTIFYING PAIN POINTS

For this exercise, you'll each want to take some alone time and allow yourselves to get introspective. During this alone time, write a list of all the things that are currently causing you pain in this relationship. Be careful not to dig up old wounds that have already been resolved; your focus should be on present-day challenges.

Once you've written down your pain points, go through and cross out any that are minor offenses and/or onetime occurrences. (Remember, we must pick and choose our battles, and if we chose to address every single offense, we'd just be sitting around trying to resolve issues all day.)

Next, look at the items that are left and rank them from most to least important. Share your top three pain points with your spouse and allow them to share their top three with you. These are the issues you'll want to focus on most as you work through this book.

Dealing with Different Perspectives

Let's say you and your spouse are out to dinner. You're sitting on one side of a table and your spouse is sitting on the other. The waiter grabs a pen and writes a number on a napkin, then places it in the middle of the table. You look at it and say, "That's a 6." Your spouse responds with confusion, "No, it's not. That's a 9." Who is correct, and who is incorrect?

What would you say to get your spouse to believe that's a 6? What could your spouse say to convince you it's a 9?

In actuality, you're both correct, because you're both seeing things from your own perspective. The way you view things in your marriage is directly related to the way you've lived your life—decisions you've made and decisions that have been made for you. So you can spend time arguing with each other, or you can walk over to your spouse's side of the table and try to see things from their point of view. To do this, you'll have to drop your defenses and get curious about why your spouse sees things so differently from you. This curiosity will lead you to a deeper understanding of how your partner's social history has affected who they are today. When you make an effort to gain that understanding, you'll be rewarded with a deeper, more intimate connection with your spouse. In other words, you'll be able to cleave to them better.

ARE YOUR VALUES IN LINE?

Our values are important because they inform the decisions we make. Your individual values often become your marriage values as you and your spouse learn to adopt each other's perspectives—or you might find yourselves constantly struggling because you simply don't understand how the other one thinks. Please use this unorthodox but very powerful values exercise to explore what you and your spouse see as important!

Thinking about death is a good way to understand what matters to us in life. To that end, I'd like you to write down in your journal or notebook what you hope people will say at your funeral. How do you want people to remember you? What accomplishments of yours do you hope they'll remember (raising children, academic achievements, career credentials, roles within the church, etc.)? Who helped you and whom did you help? What type of person would others say you were? When you're done, read your fake eulogies to each other and discuss the values that stood out to you.

Life Happens

Even when a marriage has a solid foundation, life circumstances can drive wedges between spouses. Think back to Mike and Shannon. Shannon started out with trust issues, but she and Mike were able to overcome them. They started their marriage off on healthy, loving terms. But several years and two kids later, Mike lost his job shortly after Shannon had lost her father in a car accident. They were able to live off their savings for a couple months, but then money started to get tight, and it was up to Shannon to pay all the bills. She found herself under immense pressure to perform at work so that she could keep providing for her family, all while she was grieving her father's death. She began to resent Mike and pull away emotionally. They went almost four months with little communication and no sexual intimacy due to the stress of this situation.

When life happens to you—and it will—it's important to keep things in perspective. Bad things happen to good people, just like good things happen to bad people. But God tells us that our troubles don't last forever, and that "weeping may endure for a night, but joy cometh in the morning" (Psalm 30:5, KJV). Know that although you may be struggling, God promises that it will get better. When things get rough, instead of pulling away from your spouse, push into them. Remember, the goal is to cleave to each other, even in the midst of adversity. Lean on each other so that when the situation is over, you can celebrate your strength together.

LEAVING AND CLEAVING IN SCRIPTURE
The Hebrew word used for "cleave" in Genesis 2:24 is *dabak*, and it's also used several times to talk about following God. For example, Deuteronomy 10:20 instructs us to fear, serve, and cleave to God; and Joshua 22:5 tells us to love, obey, and cleave to the Lord "with all your heart and with all your soul." The concept of leaving your parents and cleaving to your spouse as described in Genesis 2:24 is so important in scripture that Jesus quotes the verse verbatim in Matthew 19:4 and Mark 10:6.

THE FUTURE

Now that you've thought about your past and present, you can begin to look ahead to your future. Let's begin to think about your goals for your marriage as you read this book. Where do you want your relationship to go from here? What are your short-term goals for the next three months to one year? What are your long-term goals for the next five years?

Many couples I work with see goal-setting as silly or meaningless, but research tells us that creating goals, writing them down, and sharing them increases the likelihood that we'll accomplish them. One study by psychologist Dr. Gail Matthews found that writing down your goals can make you 42 percent more likely to achieve them! I want to help you not just set goals but achieve them. This book will help you do the heavy lifting and reap the benefits of a biblical marriage.

Maybe you're already thinking, "What's the point of writing down goals when there's no hope for this marriage?" Maybe you think your wife is too stubborn to change, or that your husband just wants to keep things exactly as they are. But let me tell you something: Every day that you're still married is a day when you can fight to keep your marriage and make it better.

Commitment in Christ

In Matthew 19:26, Jesus says that although righteousness is impossible for humans by ourselves, "with God all things are possible." Stay delighted in your faithfulness by believing in His Word. His Word will not return to Him void! It's vital that we keep the faith and remember that every day is a new day to hit the reset button and start again. Just as God grants us grace and mercy daily, we must work hard to grant those same gifts to our spouses.

It's so important to remember that marriage is a covenant. It's a commitment we have made not only to our spouses but to God as well. When we got married, we promised God we'd remain as one with our spouse and work at making our marriage serve Him. If we give up before we've tried everything, can we truly say that we remained faithful to our commitment of marriage?

THE THINGS THAT HOLD US BACK

There are many common challenges that can hold couples back in marriage, even when they have the best intentions. Recall that in order to plant beautiful flowers in your garden, you first have to get rid of those nasty weeds. Let's uproot some of those weeds together and plant some lovely flowers in their place.

REMEMBER YOUR WEDDING DAY

Before we discuss some common marital challenges, let's take a moment to remember the day you first started to cleave to each other. Your wedding was, I'm sure, one of the most memorable days of your life. Take some time to reflect on the day that you made your lifelong commitment to each other before God. How did you feel? What were some positive words or prayers spoken by your family and friends? What helpful advice did you receive? Write down those blessings in your journal or notebook, and return to them during the difficult times to remind yourselves of all the love and hope at the root of your marriage.

Selfishness

Let's be honest: Human beings are naturally selfish. From infancy to childhood to adolescence, we're heavily focused on our own needs and wants. Then we go into early adulthood, and we're usually responsible only for ourselves. The fact of the matter is, when you're a single person without kids, you're primarily thinking about yourself: the food you want to eat, clothes you want to wear, places you want to visit, music you want to listen to. You decide how to spend your money, when you do your laundry, and how to load your dishwasher. And guess what? That's normal and good! You're learning how to take care of your own needs.

And then you get married. Many of us actually enter marriage during the most self-centered stage of our lives. But once you exchange vows and make the commitment to your spouse to become one before God, you trade in "I" and "me" for "us" and "we." Your single vocabulary isn't the only thing that changes—so does your behavior. Now you have to compromise on the food you eat, the music you listen to, and how you spend your money. This is a joyful merging of lives, but it can also be a big adjustment.

Philippians 2:3 tells us, "Do nothing out of selfish ambition or vain conceit. Rather, in humility value others above yourselves." If you can't leave behind the self-focused behavior of singledom, it can have harmful effects on your marriage. It creates hurt feelings and a sense of disrespect. It directly affects the quality of happiness in your marriage and keeps you from being able to grow closer with your spouse. Then you have an environment ripe for resentment.

Resentment is the silent killer of marriages. It's insidious because it remains unspoken. Couples don't walk around yelling, "I resent you!" They usually don't even say the word "resent." But their actions show how resentful they are through a lack of communication, care, and patience. Keeping selfishness out of your relationship is a necessity. Replace it with compromise. When both spouses learn to put each other's needs before their own wants, they create a marriage based on selflessness.

Keeping Up with the Joneses

Remember that when you work on your marriage with a tool like this book, you're trying to help your marriage grow—not compare it to other people's. We live in a social media world where people can fabricate any "relationship," real or fake, and convince people they're living a life they're not. On any given day, you can log in to Facebook or Instagram and see what people call "#RelationshipGoals." You see the couple who wears matching sweatshirts or takes the most expensive vacations or has the cutest kids. Seeing these pictures can trick us into thinking we're missing out on something that other people have, and that if we just made more money or worked harder, we'd have the perfect marriage.

Well, let me be the first to tell you: There is no perfect marriage, so save your energy, stress, and effort. Try to reach your *own* standards. Decide what you want for *your* marriage and set goals for yourselves, individually and as a couple. Then work as a team toward those goals. You can even schedule monthly check-ins that let you hold each other accountable when you get off track and celebrate when you make progress. We all have the marriage we've created—and that means we can create new circumstances at any point.

Think About How You Think

Even without social media, most of us have a picture in our heads of what marriage should be. We went into marriage with certain expectations of what it would feel and look like. The question is: What sources from our own experiences and life histories have most influenced our expectations? The media? Our parents or extended families? Social norms?

Do we believe the expectations instilled in us by outside influences are right for us, or have we just been told to abide by them?

When we ask ourselves these types of questions, we're thinking about *how* and *why* we think the things we do, which is called "metacognitive thinking." According to Nancy Chick, the assistant director of Vanderbilt University's Center for Teaching, this helps us "become aware of [our] strengths and weaknesses." She goes on to say that when you understand the origins of your knowledge and ability, it's easier to "expand that knowledge or extend that ability." Thinking about how you think will empower you with a strong understanding of what influences you most, what beliefs about marriage you truly want to foster, and which ideas and approaches work best for your relationship. This type of mental housekeeping will help you take control of your future and set you up for the best in your marriage.

Setting aside what your history or influences tell you, do you believe you can be a good wife or husband? Do you believe you can resolve conflict with your spouse? Do you believe you have the ability to stay faithful? You must work toward answering these additional questions with a resounding "Yes!" Remember, for your greatest success, the expectations within your marriage should be created by you and your partner *and* aligned with the Word of God.

Getting Tangled in Thoughts

Just as we guard ourselves from negative behaviors, we must also guard ourselves from negative thoughts. A school of therapy called cognitive behavioral therapy (CBT) teaches that thoughts are just thoughts—nothing more, nothing less. It can be detrimental to give the wrong thoughts power over our lives. We especially shouldn't let negative thoughts control us or hinder us from reaching our potential. We often limit our own ability to change, grow, and evolve in marriage just because we believe a negative thought like "I married the wrong person" or "We'll never see eye to eye."

We have to learn to recognize false or negative thoughts as false or negative thoughts. Then we can change them to more positive and useful thoughts. Allowing our thoughts to control our behavior hinders us from doing what God wants. As Romans 12:2 says, "Do not conform to the pattern of this world, but be transformed by the renewing of your mind."

GIVE YOUR SUFFERING OVER TO HIM

If you feel stuck in your marriage, like you can never get ahead or move on to the next level, remember that God wants us to cast our cares upon Him. He has promised never to leave us or forsake us. In Isaiah 43:2, He says, "When you pass through the waters, I will be with you; and when you pass through the rivers, they will not sweep over you. When you walk through the fire, you will not be burned." And Romans 5:3–5 adds, "We also glory in our sufferings, because we know that suffering produces persever-ance; perseverance, character; and character, hope." So remain encouraged! Your struggle has not been in vain. I truly believe that God can see you through the hard times and lead you to a better place in your marriage. Meanwhile, as you and your spouse do the difficult work to get there, know that He will be with you.

WHERE DO WE GO FROM HERE?

Now that we've taken a broad look at your marriage's past, present, and future, where do we go from here? Here's what the rest of the chapters in this book will cover.

CHAPTER TWO: The Communication Key

This chapter covers communication with your spouse in all its forms, from common pitfalls to the importance of non-verbal communication to biblical communication principles. We'll go over the importance of honesty and directness, which, when coupled with compassion and sensitivity, let us talk with our spouses with genuine intimacy. You'll also complete some exercises to help you improve your communication skills as well as redirect the negative thoughts that might be stymieing the way you converse with your partner.

CHAPTER THREE: Fair Fights

Conflict isn't always bad! You can fight with your spouse in ways that are healthy, respectful, and Christian. This chapter will teach you how. First we'll look at ways to resolve a disagreement before it flares into a fight, then we'll discuss how to fight fair, and finally we'll examine how to recover from a fight and learn to do a little better next time.

CHAPTER FOUR: Intimacy

Intimacy is crucial to any couple's well-being—and I'm not just talking about sex. Emotional intimacy is the most important form of intimacy and acts as a foundation for all other forms, including physical. But, yes, this chapter will also discuss sex and how to approach issues in your sex life with directness and compassion, including exercises to help you rekindle romance and restore intimacy.

CHAPTER FIVE: Team Up

Marriage is best when approached as a team sport. Though it may sometimes feel like you and your spouse are going head-to-head, try to understand that you're teammates who must work together in order to win. This chapter is all about how to share responsibilities, challenges, and victories as members of the same team, with exercises that will enable you to serve and uplift your partner when they're struggling.

CHAPTER SIX: Dealing with Difficult Conditions

We've explored the more common issues faced in many marriages, but what if you have an even bigger problem to deal with, like infidelity, addiction, or mental illness? This chapter will tackle those difficult conditions and how to handle them.

CHAPTER SEVEN: Rebuilding Trust

Trust is fundamental to any relationship. This chapter explores rebuilding trust—the key to true emotional intimacy with your spouse—even after the kinds of difficult conditions explored in chapter 6. The goal is to help you and your partner have enough trust to lead connected but independent lives, even if there is betrayal in your history together. By strengthening the trust in your relationship, you and your partner can experience the ultimate goal for your marriage: *agape* love—the purest form of unconditional love, the kind God has for us.

COMMITTED ACTION

We've covered a lot of ground in this first chapter, but I want to make sure you have a few tools in your toolbox that you can put to use right away.

1. Go ahead and engage in a conversation with your spouse about the concept of leaving and cleaving. Begin to hash out any challenges you may have around this. Remember that learning to leave old perspectives and patterns behind is a process, and we can't do it all at once.

2. Remember the pain points you wrote down earlier? I want you to pick one identified by your spouse and start creating a "prescription" for it. Begin to work on being a healing place for your spouse.

3. Consider what thoughts came up for you as you read about the concept of selfishness on page 12. Identify three areas in your marriage where you could be less selfish. For each one, think of one action you can take to counteract that selfishness with compromise.

Do not let any unwholesome talk come out of your mouths, but only what is helpful for building others up according to their needs, that it may benefit those who listen.

Ephesians 4:29

CHAPTER TWO

THE COMMUNICATION KEY

COMMUNICATION IS THE FOUNDATION of every relationship we have as humans, so naturally it's going to be fundamental to a successful marriage. In my private practice, communication challenges are the number one reason I see couples. This chapter will discuss why healthy communication is so crucial and how improving your communication will help you solve many other relationship problems.

COMMON COMMUNICATION PITFALLS

I don't think there exists a married couple that hasn't succumbed to a communication pitfall. Because communication is something we do day in and day out, it stands to reason that we're likely to make mistakes at it every now and then. Some couples don't communicate enough, keeping their thoughts and feelings to themselves and never working out their issues. Some communicate in unhealthy ways, with constant arguing or hurtful words. And most of us are much fonder of being heard than we are of listening. One of the things that I teach couples during therapy is that we must learn to listen with the intention not merely to respond but to really understand. As Proverbs 18:2 says, "Fools find no pleasure in understanding but delight in airing their own opinions."

For Rob and Estela, communication has broken down in their relationship. They both struggle with this in different ways. Estela often speaks in absolutes, accusing Rob of "always" doing this or "never" doing that. Meanwhile, Rob has a habit of shutting down and not sharing his thoughts or emotions at all when he's frustrated. Rob feels like whenever he opens his mouth to speak, Estela is waiting to attack him, and that keeps him from wanting to speak at all.

Let's examine some of the more common communication pitfalls more closely and see if any sound familiar to you.

How does a typical conversation go between you and your spouse? Does one person do most of the talking and the other most of the listening, or is it about even? Do you come out of the conversations feeling understood, or do you feel like they've missed your point? Does your partner make eye contact with you or otherwise indicate that they're tuned in and paying attention to what you're saying? Is there mutual understanding of what's being said on both sides? If you can't come to an agreement on something, are you able to agree to disagree? Write down your answers to these questions as well as any other thoughts that come up. Keep them in mind as you read this chapter.

"You" and "I"

When communicating with your spouse, especially during a conflict, it's important to express what you're feeling with an "I" statement rather than accusing them of something with a "you" statement. What are "I" statements and "you" statements?

A "you" statement is a sentence that describes what your spouse is feeling, thinking, or doing, and it often starts with the word "you." Some examples of "you" statements include:

- You never include me in your weekend plans. You'd rather spend time with your friends than with me.
- You just want to argue every time I bring up money.
- You think you're so high and mighty, but you're not.

The problem with these kinds of statements is that you're not inside your spouse's head, and you may have their thoughts and feelings all wrong. We're always speaking from our own perspectives, but instead of acknowledging this, "you" statements place the blame on the other person.

An "I" statement, on the other hand, usually starts with a phrase like "I feel" or "I think." It lets you express your thoughts and feelings from your point of view, without putting words in the other person's mouth. Examples of healthy "I" statements include:

- **I feel neglected** when you hang out with your friends during a time I wanted you to hang out with me.
- **I feel stressed out** when we talk about money right before bed, so I'd like to have this conversation tomorrow instead.
- **I feel loved** when you ask me for my opinion on something before taking action on it.

The Problem, Not the Person

While we're on the subject of using "I," not "you," let's also remember to focus on the problem, not the person. If you have an issue with your spouse's behavior, you have an issue with that behavior—not with your spouse as a person. Whether you realize it or not, when you say something like "You're so lazy," you're attacking who your spouse is. This can damage not only your spouse's self-esteem but your relationship as well. Instead, try saying something like "I would really like if you went grocery shopping today instead of putting it off until tomorrow." That's focusing on the problem, not the person. It doesn't damage the trust or bond between you, and your spouse will likely be more willing to modify a problematic behavior when they don't feel under attack.

Pay Attention

There's nothing worse than talking to someone with their face buried in their phone or glued to the TV. One of the easiest ways to offend your spouse is to not give them the attention they deserve during conversations or quality time. This can be challenging in the age of technology, when there are so many things that distract us from our families. I advocate for meals and quality time without phones or TVs, so people can give their spouses the eye contact and full attention they deserve.

I always say there's a difference between listening with your ears and listening with your heart. When you listen with your ears, you may hear the words coming out of your spouse's mouth, but you're not engaging with them genuinely. When you listen with your heart, you're taking the time to really understand them and respond thoughtfully.

Passive-Aggression

Passive-aggressive behavior seems peaceful on the surface, but it's actually a form of covert aggression. Think about Rob and Estela. You may recall that Rob has trouble speaking up. When he's frustrated with something Estela is doing, instead of addressing it directly, he resorts to passive-aggression. Let's say it's Estela's turn to do the dishes, but she doesn't do them. Maybe she forgot, maybe she's too busy, or maybe she's slacking off—Rob doesn't know because he doesn't ask her about it. Instead, as the dishes pile up, Rob finds himself feeling angrier and angrier. He's "passive" in that he doesn't take action. He doesn't argue about it or wash the dishes himself. But he's "aggressive" in that he lets the conflict grow and grow without resolving it. Inevitably, his frustration will come out in a different way that will be unfair to Estela. Maybe she'll make an offhand comment and he'll accuse her of being inconsiderate and lazy, or maybe he'll give her the cold shoulder and she won't understand why. That's how passive-aggression works.

Passive-aggressive behavior is common among married couples, and it usually doesn't happen out of direct malice. Rather, it stems from living in a selfish space. Ironically, people who are acting this way often think they're being selfless because they're avoiding conflict or sparing their spouse their emotions, but it's actually quite the opposite. Not sharing your feelings and heart with your spouse is selfish behavior. It can also be very confusing when you end up expressing your hurt or anger through your behavior rather than your words and your spouse doesn't understand why.

Directives and Ultimatums

Communication is a two-way exchange of information. If you communicate only by issuing directives (telling your spouse what to do) or ultimatums (telling your spouse that if they don't do something you want them to do, you'll retaliate in some way), you don't leave much room for your spouse to participate. It makes you a dictator rather than a teammate in conversation.

Ultimatums and directives can be dangerous for relationships because they make your spouse feel trapped or forced to do things against their will, which causes resentment and breaks down trust. Instead of using these tactics, approach your spouse with openness, vulnerability, and respect.

One strategy I teach my couples is based on relationship researcher John Gottman's concept of the "dream detective." When your spouse tries to give you an ultimatum or directive, can you figure out their underlying feeling, desire, or "dream" and come up with a better way to address it?

Let's look at an example. When Will and Suzanne had been dating seriously for a while, Will tried to use an ultimatum. Here's how the conversation went:

WILL: *We've been dating for a year. Why don't you want to get married yet? If we don't get engaged in the next six months, I'm going to leave and find someone else who's more ready for marriage.*

SUZANNE: *Stop trying to force me into marriage! I'm not going to get married until I feel ready!*

Later, Suzanne decided to work on being a dream detective to figure out why Will was feeling this way.

SUZANNE: *Why is getting married so important to you? Are you afraid that I don't want to be with you?*

WILL: *When I was young, my father walked away from my family. Without him around, my siblings and I fell out of touch as we got older. I feel like I lost everyone I loved. Now that I have you in my life, I never want to lose you. I love and care for you deeply. I want to be with you forever, and I want you to feel the same way.*

It still took a while for Suzanne to feel ready for marriage, but she and Will were able to talk about it more openly. Will felt less scared of losing Suzanne and didn't try to coerce her by using an ultimatum again.

NONVERBAL COMMUNICATION

Nonverbal communication is any communication that happens without words, such as facial expressions, body language, or gestures. If your arms are crossed and your brow is furrowed, you may be indicating that you're angry. If you maintain eye contact during an important conversation, you're showing that you're paying attention. You say all this without ever speaking a word.

Reading Your Spouse's Body Language

When talking to your spouse, you can listen to both the words they're saying and what they're telling you with their body. This will help you communicate more effectively. For example, if your partner is talking to you about adding some excitement to your sex life, and you notice that their leg is shaking and they're not making direct eye contact with you as they talk, you might conclude that they're nervous or embarrassed. You can then respond by putting a hand on their knee to reassure them or telling them verbally, "It's okay if you're nervous. I'm listening."

Here are the five most common examples of body language I see in my private practice during tense or difficult conversations:

1. **Eye rolling.** Nothing says "Whatever, I don't take this seriously," like an eye roll.

2. **Crossed arms.** This gesture indicates someone is feeling defensive or closed off.

3. **Shaky leg(s).** This is usually a sign of nervousness or irritability.

4. **Deep sighs or huffs.** This indicates resentment or frustration, almost as if to say, "Here we go again."

5. **Speaking under your breath.** Why does speaking count as body language? Because most of the time when people mutter, they don't necessarily mean for the other person to hear the words they're saying. Instead they're communicating that they're not listening or don't care.

When your spouse exhibits one of these types of body language, you may be confused, hurt, or angry. You may feel like getting defensive and rolling your eyes or crossing your arms right back. But a great response could simply be acknowledging that your spouse seems off. You can ask them how they feel, offer to give them a hug, or even give them space until they're more relaxed and ready to communicate.

Reading Your Own Body Language

You may be able to recognize what your spouse is telling you with their body, but can you recognize what your own body is telling you? Paying attention to your own body's physical cues is just as essential as paying attention to your spouse's. Can you recognize when your body is telling you that you're frustrated, angry, hurt, or anxious? Maybe your heart rate increases, your shoulders hunch up, your palms sweat, or your breathing changes. Maybe you start to cry.

Be vigilant when your body sends these messages. They make it harder for you to communicate with your spouse, both verbally and nonverbally. You might be more inclined to say something hurtful or shut down the conversation non-verbally by rolling your eyes or turning away. If you notice you're feeling these sensations, try taking deep breaths from your belly or calling for a time-out and spending a few moments alone—whatever you need to get back into a headspace where you can communicate openly and honestly without being emotionally overwhelmed.

The Biblical View

I tell my couples all the time that it's not what you say but how you say it that truly matters. When you're communicating with your spouse, take note of the volume and tone of your voice, and leave any sarcasm to the children. Colossians 4:6 says, "Let your conversation be always full of grace, seasoned with salt, so that you may know how to answer everyone." And, yes, "everyone" includes your spouse! God wants us to be good stewards of even our words. He doesn't want us to waste them being mean or sarcastic—He wants our words to drip with love and compassion!

CONFLICT COMMUNICATION STYLES

How do you communicate during a conflict with your spouse? There are a few common styles.

- **An aggressive or competitive style** gives a high regard to self and a low regard to others. People using this style try to "win" the conflict, sometimes by any means necessary, but they end up being in a lose/lose situation, because a loss for either individual in a marriage is a loss for the couple as a whole. In marriage, we win and we lose together.
- **An accommodating, passive, or submissive style** is the opposite of aggressive, with a low regard for the self but a high regard for others. Sometimes it's appropriate to be accommodating, but when one spouse makes a habit of it, their needs may consistently go unmet. It

may seem selfless, but again, if it hurts the marriage overall, it hurts both individuals in the marriage.

- **An avoidant style** indicates a low regard for both self and others. People using this style try to avoid conflict or difficult communication altogether. The problem is that we're never *not* communicating. You may not be saying much, but your emotions will end up coming out in other ways. A marriage with healthy conflicts is much healthier than a marriage where all conflicts are avoided.

- **A collaborative style** is what you want to aim for. This style shows a high degree of concern for both self and others, taking each spouse's point of view into account and working as a team to resolve conflicts. Although this style takes the most time and effort, it also creates the strongest relationship and ultimately the most harmony and happiness.

PRINCIPLES OF CHRISTIAN COMMUNICATION

When talking about communication in a Christian marriage, it's essential to remember the third member of your marriage: God. Communication is more than just our ability to talk; it's also our ability to listen. As we communicate with God, we must pray, but we must also listen. The primary way we can listen to God is by reading His Word, and the Bible gives us clear guidelines on communication. James 1:19 says, "My dear brothers, take note of this: Everyone should be quick to listen, slow to speak and slow to become angry." When we speak in anger, we fail to obey God's commands or show God's love.

Now, I know this can be easier said than done, especially when it comes to our spouses, but it's what God calls for us to do. During our communication with God through prayer, we can ask for the ability to live out His will. We can ask God for the patience it takes to communicate with our spouse properly.

Being able to see the good in our spouses will also help us to be slow to anger, because it helps us to "err on the positive" or give our spouses the benefit of the doubt. For example, if you ask your spouse to grab something from the store on their way home from work, but they forget, you have two choices. You could "err on the positive" and say, "I know you had a long day at work and probably just forgot to stop." On the other hand, you could "err on the negative" and say, "You don't view my needs as important! You don't care enough about me to get what I asked you to get." Your response can go either way, but if you want to go in the way that pleases God and best serves your marriage, you'll be patient and slow to anger. Now let's look at some other important principles of Christian communication.

Speak the Truth

Colossians 3:9 puts it simply: "Do not lie to each other." A healthy marriage is built on trust. Trust is built on honesty. It's so important that we be honest with each other by speaking our truth without exaggerating or equivocating. Many times, couples aren't honest with each other because they're afraid they'll hurt their spouse's feelings or anger their spouse. However, all that withholding truth ultimately does is create a bed of resentment for your partner to sleep in.

Remember how Rob often withholds his truth and pretends not to feel a certain way because he doesn't want Estela to attack him? In the short term, he may be able to avoid a confrontation, but in the long term, Estela just grows more and more frustrated because she doesn't understand where he's coming from and doesn't trust him to be able to talk about it. That means that she's actually *more* likely to lash out at him, not less. Honesty might hurt your spouse's feelings sometimes, even when it's delivered with compassion. But that doesn't mean it's better to be dishonest.

Deal with Problems Head-On

Ephesians 4:26–27 says, "'In your anger do not sin': Do not let the sun go down while you are still angry, and do not give the devil a foothold." Now, there's a time and place for everything, and I'm not suggesting you address problems while out to dinner with your friends or at a parent-teacher conference. Nor am I suggesting you be cruel or aggressive. But I am suggesting you be direct and deal with your anger instead of letting it fester.

Once you're in the correct environment for conflict resolution, here are some guidelines for addressing your conflict directly but compassionately.

1. Make sure you're on the same page. Define the specific conflict and both spouses' concerns. (Sometimes you might find that you think you're arguing about one thing, while your spouse thinks you're arguing about another.)

2. Once you know you're on the same page, use your "I" statements (see page 24) and take turns expressing how you feel.

3. If any apologies need to be made, make them! This step may be uncomfortable, but I encourage you to embrace the discomfort and do it anyway.

4. Focus on solutions. Even if you're still frustrated with each other, agreeing on a solution will prevent your mind from dwelling on negative feelings toward your spouse, which "gives the devil a foothold." You don't necessarily have to find a solution literally before the sun goes down, but agreeing to do it sooner than later is most effective.

Think Before You Speak

Proverbs 16:23 says, "Intelligent people think before they speak" (GNT). As we have explored, the Bible advises us to be honest and direct in our communication, but when we do so without thinking, we can be hurtful. When we're intentional with our words, on the other hand, our honesty builds trust and intimacy. Most of the unintentional hurt that comes about during communication happens because we speak first and think later. We just spew out words from a place of painful feelings in that moment. But when we're truthful *and* sensitive, we can communicate the way God wants us to.

The "One Anothers"

There are many places in the Bible that tell us how to treat one another.

Be kind and compassionate to one another, forgiving each other, just as in Christ God forgave you.
Ephesians 4:32

Accept one another, then, just as Christ accepted you, in order to bring praise to God.
Romans 15:7

Therefore confess your sins to each other and pray for each other that you may be healed.
James 5:16

What power there is in these scriptures, especially when we apply them to marriage. God forgave us, so we and our spouses forgive one another. God accepts us, so we and our spouses accept one another. And when we confess our sins and pray together, communicating with each other and with God, we become vulnerable with each other, which allows us to experience true emotional intimacy and genuinely pray for each other's healing.

DEALING WITH HARD THOUGHTS

I mentioned in chapter 1 that cognitive behavioral therapy (CBT) is a common type of "talk therapy." I use it in my practice to help couples become aware of their negative or irrational thinking habits. Thoughts are simply thoughts until we act on them, and understanding the basics of CBT helps couples take control over their thoughts. If you accept that you're in control over your thoughts, you can accept that you can defuse and change them. It's like Philippians 4:8 says: "Finally, brothers and sisters, whatever is true, whatever is noble, whatever is right, whatever is pure, whatever is lovely, whatever is admirable—if anything is excellent or praiseworthy—think about such things."

Letting Go of Negative Thoughts

It's important to know that just because a thought is passing through your mind, that doesn't mean you have to own that thought or devalue yourself because of it. When you find yourself having a negative thought, you can observe the thought, acknowledge it, and then change it. For example, let's say you think, "My spouse doesn't compliment me after I cook dinner. I must be a terrible cook." In all likelihood, you're not a terrible cook and your spouse enjoys your cooking. Maybe they feel that eating the meal you made is the way to show appreciation for your cooking, or maybe they just don't know that you want to hear a compliment now and then. You don't know, so don't dwell on the negative thought and make it your reality.

How do you approach letting go of negative thoughts?

1. Remind yourself that you are not your thoughts. Thoughts arise in our minds all the time. Sometimes they're brilliant and insightful; sometimes they're completely nonsensical. Detaching from these thoughts helps you understand that they're perfectly natural but not permanent.

2. Think about where this thought comes from. Is it the voice of an insecurity you have about your abilities or worth? Is it a cruel remark someone once made to you? You might even just be in a bad mood.

3. Put a smile on your face. Negative thoughts often cause the kind of negative nonverbal communication

we discussed on page 29, like crossed arms, hunched shoulders, or a frown. But research shows it works the other way, too: If you uncross your arms, relax your shoulders, and let yourself smile a little, it helps put you in a positive state of mind.

4. Talk back to your thoughts. If the little voice in your head tells you something negative, think up a positive response. You can even say it out loud. Be patient and honest with yourself as you come up with a rebuttal to those negative words.

You're in control of your thoughts! The sooner you begin to practice this self-control, the sooner your negative thoughts can be a thing of the past.

CHANGE YOUR SELF-TALK

During my marriage retreats, I use this exercise to help couples change their negative self-talk. Here's what you do:

1. Get a piece of paper and draw a vertical line down the middle. Label the left side "Negative Thoughts" and the right side "Positive Thoughts."

2. In the left column, list everything negative you think about your marriage, your spouse, or yourself.

3. Once your list is complete, move to the right side of the page and write a rebuttal to each negative thought. For example, if you wrote "Sex with my spouse has become boring" in the left-hand column, you might write, "Our sex life isn't where I want it to be right now, but I can start a conversation about making it more exciting" on the right.

If you think of more negative thoughts, you can continue to add them, but make sure you always come up with a rebuttal. You can repeat this exercise anytime you want to change a negative thought.

LET GOD GUIDE YOU

I get it, I get it. You're probably thinking that changing your thoughts is easier said than done, especially if you've built up a habit of negative thinking for most of your life. But let me remind you that you're not alone. As long as you have faith, there's nothing you can't accomplish with Christ. Let us be reminded of Peter in Matthew 14. Peter was ready to test his faith, so he asked Jesus to tell him to walk on water. When Jesus said, "Come," Peter immediately got out of the boat and proceeded toward Jesus. His faith was strong enough to walk on water . . . until he felt a strong wind and began to feel fear, pressure, and doubt. Then he began to sink under the waves.

Let's think about these negative perceptions in terms of marriage. The second you begin to feel fear, pressure, and doubt, it changes your perception of your spouse and your marriage. When Peter allowed those kinds of thoughts to affect him and took his focus off God, he lost faith and began to sink. But something miraculous happened. He cried out to Jesus for help. Jesus immediately grabbed his hand and saved him, but He told Peter that he needed more faith.

See, God never gives up on us. Despite the fact that Peter didn't have enough faith in that moment, Jesus still used him as the rock on which to build the church. Even if we mess up, we can always try again, and God still has a plan for us. When you find yourself struggling to change your thoughts and perceptions about your spouse or your marriage, cry out to God and allow Him to reach out His hand and pull you up from the depths.

NONVIOLENT COMMUNICATION

Proverbs 15:4 says, "The soothing tongue is a tree of life, but a perverse tongue crushes the spirit." This biblical concept is reflected in the principles of nonviolent communication developed by the psychologist Marshall Rosenberg. Violent communication is communication that cuts deeply—name-calling, cruel words you know will hurt your spouse, intentionally twisting your spouse's words, focusing only on the negative. Nonviolent communication, on the other hand, helps you get in touch with your own needs, which in turn helps you see the needs of your spouse. When your words are kinder and softer, your spouse will be better able to hear and understand what you're saying, and vice versa.

There are four components to using nonviolent communication:

1. **Observations:** What is happening around you? What do you see and hear?

2. **Feelings:** How do you feel as a result of the things you observe?

3. **Desires:** What do you need, value, or want as a result of what you observe and how it makes you feel?

4. **Requests:** What specific requests can you make to help resolve the situation?

Here's an example of how this might play out:

1. **Observation:** I just had a very nasty fight with my wife. I said some pretty mean things to her and even called her a name that caused her to cry. She said some mean things to me too, including that she wants a divorce.

2. **Feelings:** I feel horrible and guilty. I'm embarrassed by my behavior. I feel pretty low right now.

3. **Desires:** What I wanted to do was have a conversation about my wife's spending habits and how they affect our mutual finances, but I just caused an argument I regret. I want to fix that. I only meant to share my feelings, not hurt my wife.

4. Requests: Tonight, I'll make dinner and ask her to forgive me. Then I'll ask for us to try the conversation again with better communication skills so we can be on the same page about how we manage our money.

As you can see, using nonviolent communication is introspective and sometimes difficult work, but it can completely change your communication dynamics for the better.

INFORMAL COMMUNICATION

If you and your spouse are struggling with communication, you may find that starting with simple, informal conversations helps. Begin with light topics. Ask about your spouse's day, the local news, or happenings at work—but instead of just nodding your head in response to what your spouse says, ask more questions and keep the conversation going. You may not be talking about deep topics, but you're still building a deeper connection.

Here's an example of what I'm talking about.

TRINA: *How was your day at work, honey?*

JIM: *Pretty stressful.*

TRINA: *How so? Tell me more.*

JIM: *Well, the company is going through some changes, and my boss is being promoted, which means I'll have a new boss starting next week.*

TRINA: *Next week? That seems like a pretty quick turnaround! How do you feel about it?*

JIM: *I feel rushed. I only learned about it today. I prefer to have time to adjust to new people, so this will be hard for me. It's giving me some anxiety.*

See how that simple "How was your day?" turned into an opportunity to share emotions and connect on a deeper level? Try working this approach into your everyday communication, and put it on repeat!

COMMUNICATION THROUGH CHRIST

The couple that prays together stays together. For this exercise, I challenge you to pick a topic and pray on it together with your partner. You could take turns within the same prayer, or you could pray individually one after the other. For example, let's say you're praying about money.

One of you could start by thanking God for the funds you currently have, using this time to "enter his gates with thanksgiving and his courts with praise" (Psalm 100:4). Next, the other spouse could make any requests you have about your finances known, then close it out with thanks again and seal it in faith. However you want to do it is fine, just as long as you both have input in the prayer.

After your prayer is over, share with your spouse about how you feel. Do you feel more unified? Do you feel closer? Is communicating through Christ together something you want to adopt on a regular basis?

COMMITTED ACTION

We took a deeper look at communication in this chapter, and I hope you feel more prepared to communicate using some of the techniques we covered. Here are the top three things I want to make sure you take away and apply to your marriage right now:

1. Set aside some time to practice the "dream detective" strategy. Ask your spouse their dreams and aspirations, and use the strategy to explore and learn more.

2. Assess your current communication to see how much you're actively practicing Christian principles. Take a piece of paper and draw a vertical line down the middle. On one side, write down the ways you currently communicate, and on the other side, write down the Christian principles you hope to adopt for your communications. Choose two of the principles that you'll begin to implement right away.

3. Practice nonviolent communication beginning today. Use all four steps (see pages 43–44) during your next conversation about needs with your spouse.

And the Lord's servant must not be quarrelsome but must be kind to everyone, able to teach, not resentful.

2 Timothy 2:24

CHAPTER THREE

FAIR FIGHTS

TO BE IN A MARRIAGE WITHOUT ANY FIGHTS is every person's dream but not many people's reality. As a matter of fact, fighting can be a very healthy component of any relationship. When they're handled the right way, fights can help us get through challenging times and make us stronger together. Now that we've covered some essential communication tools, let's put them to use and learn how to fight fair.

FOUR COMMON FIGHTS

Job 15:3 asks, "Would they argue with useless words, with speeches that have no value?" If we're being honest, the sad but true answer is "Yes, we have, and we'll do it again." Couples fight for many reasons, but there are a few common issues that come up for many or most couples. These include money, children, in-laws, and sex (or the lack thereof). These topics can be major hot buttons for even the strongest couples. Let's break them down.

Money

According to a study by finance writer Dave Ramsey's company Ramsey Solutions, money is "the number one issue married couples argue about" and "money fights are the second leading cause of divorce, behind infidelity." Have you ever heard the saying that there's his side, her side, and the truth? Well, the same could be said about a couple's finances. Many couples have different perspectives on managing money, and that causes problems in their marriages. For our purposes, let's not focus on "his views on money" or "her views on money." Let's focus on the mutual conversations about money that make for a healthy marriage. Here are a few strategies for dealing with conflict around finances in a healthy way, even when you disagree with each other.

TALK WHEN YOU'RE NOT IN CRISIS

The best time to communicate about money problems is when you're not right in the middle of a money problem. If you only discuss your finances when an unexpected crisis comes up, your conversations will be fraught with emotions and tensions. You're more likely to feel defensive, blame each other, and not listen to what the other person has to say.

To achieve this, set a time every month for conversations around income, expenses, savings, and financial goals for your family. When these discussions are intentional and planned, it's easier to make rational decisions together as a team. Even the Bible tells us this in Luke 14:28: "Suppose one of you wants to build a tower. Won't you first sit down and estimate the cost to see if you have enough money to complete it?" (Dave Ramsey isn't the only money expert—the Word gives us guidance on everything!)

BE SPECIFIC

A lot of our money challenges occur because of miscommunication and misunderstanding. Being clear and specific about money leaves little room for confusion. When we understand exactly what the other person means, we can have more productive conversations about money.

Lisa and Kerlin, for example, argue about money a lot. They've divided up the bills between them such that Kerlin pays the four largest bills in the household (the mortgage, car insurance, and both car payments), while Lisa covers all the rest of the smaller bills (utilities, the phone plan, and so on). Whenever they fight—and they fight a lot—Lisa ends up saying something like, "I'm paying all the bills, so I should have more say." Kerlin responds, "No way—I pay all the bills! Without me paying the mortgage, we wouldn't even have a place to live!"

What Kerlin doesn't realize is that all the small bills that Lisa pays add up to a lot of money, and that it requires some extra work for her to keep track of all those different expenditures. What Lisa doesn't realize is that Kerlin carries some extra stress about the major bills he's responsible for, because if he falls behind on payments for the house or cars, it could affect the couple's life together in significant ways. If the couple talked about those specifics, they might be able to understand each other's perspectives better and come up with a solution. Saying something vague like "I pay all the bills around here" just causes more stress and conflict.

GET OUT OF DEBT

God wants us to "let no debt remain outstanding, except the continuing debt to love one another" (Romans 13:8). He can't use us to bless others financially if we're not properly managing our own money. In today's economy, it's often impossible to be 100 percent debt-free, but if you both prioritize paying off as much debt as possible, you'll not only benefit financially, you'll also benefit relationship-wise by being on the same page and sharing a goal. As Deuteronomy 28:12 says, when the Lord opens "the storehouse of his bounty . . . to bless the work of your hands," you "will lend to many nations but will borrow from none."

Children

Co-parenting can be challenging for many couples, especially if you don't communicate about it *before* becoming parents. Parenting requires much "pre-communication": ahead-of-time conversations about the children's education, health, and other aspects of daily life. For example, you and your spouse should discuss your views on your child dating long before they're old enough to date. If you haven't had children yet, the time to have these conversations is now, but be flexible and take into account that as you learn more about life with kids, you may change some of your parenting viewpoints. Put these conversations on repeat now and continue to have them even after children arrive. If you are already a parent, pre-communicate regularly.

When you find yourselves fighting about parenting, make sure to do so when the kids aren't present. Go to a separate room or wait until you're alone to discuss major decisions. When you've come to a decision, present it to your children together as a united front. Until then, you can ask your children for patience as you consult with your spouse. It's more important for your kids to know you and your spouse are on the same team than for them to get an immediate answer on an issue. They should be able to trust that your plans for them are something you and your spouse mutually agreed on (even if you're both compromising on what you originally wanted).

Family

Our families of origin can be the source of many conflicts with our spouses. Does one of you have a parent who thinks they can tell you how to raise your kids? Is one of you caring for elderly parents, with all the additional stress that entails? Does your spouse's family just not seem to like you very much? These are all common sources of fights for married couples. These conflicts can be extra tricky because when you have a problem with your partner's family of origin, your partner can feel like you have a problem with who they are and where they came from. Keep that in mind when trying to fight fair. But also remember the importance of leaving and cleaving, as discussed in chapter 1. Just as you present a united front to your kids, you must also present a united front to your families.

Let's go back to Lisa and Kerlin for a moment. When Lisa's sister lost her job and needed a small loan, Lisa gave it to her without hesitation and didn't communicate about it with Kerlin. It was just a onetime thing, and it didn't seem worth mentioning. But then one loan request turned into two, and two turned into three. Lisa realized she had started a bad trend. Proverbs 6 tell us that "the Lord hates . . . a lying tongue," so the first thing Lisa needed to do was confess to her husband. She told him what had been going on and apologized for not being honest. Next they sat down and got on the same page about Lisa's sister. They discussed stopping the loans completely but eventually decided to keep lending her a smaller amount of money with an organized plan to pay it back when she was able to find employment again. They could have come up with other ways to address the problem, too—what's important is that they decided together.

Sex

Sex is another common source of conflict for couples. Maybe one partner has a higher libido than the other, or maybe both want to have sex more often but are too busy with kids and jobs to find time. This can be a very sensitive subject and difficult to talk about. For that reason, I'll devote the entire next chapter to sex and intimacy, so I won't go into detail about it here just yet.

WHAT DO YOU FIGHT ABOUT?

Set aside some time with your partner to discuss what you fight about most often. Each of you should write down a list of five things in your journal or notebook. (You can draw from the four common fights we just explored, but you certainly don't have to.)

When you're done, compare lists and circle any items you both wrote down. Why do you think those are the things you fight about most? What about those topics is sensitive? What acts as a trigger? Have you tried to talk about them before? Journal your thoughts, then discuss.

This conversation will likely bring up strong emotions, so tread lightly. Speak honestly but compassionately. Speak your truth genuinely and listen with the same degree of genuineness. Be kind with your words and actively try not to trigger each other. If you feel yourself getting angry or worked up, take a break and try again on a different day.

STOP FIGHTING BEFORE IT STARTS

Often in arguments, we feed off each other's words and energy. We become determined to have the last word, to deliver the meanest comeback, to prove we're right and our spouses are wrong. We end up hurting our spouses, ourselves, and our marriages. When we start to feel riled up, how can we stop the situation from getting out of hand? The key is not to just avoid the conflict, which allows bad feelings to fester and leads to worse conflicts later on. Instead, make use of these strategies.

Be Curious

Ask yourself: What are we fighting about? Are we really fighting over the fact that I bought the wrong brand of cereal at the store, or are we fighting over something much deeper, like the fact that my spouse feels I don't take their requests seriously? Is this fight worth it? Am I picking and choosing my battles? Are we fighting about the same thing, or are we experiencing two different problems? Be genuinely curious about figuring out the root of the problem rather than trying to "win" the fight. When you start to get answers to these questions, keep asking more until you're both totally clear about what your partner is trying to communicate.

Be Slow to Speak

James 1:19 reminds us to be quick to listen and slow to become angry. This instruction can't be stressed enough. When you and your spouse disagree on something, don't go right into fighting mode. Stop and consider your words carefully. The benefit of pausing before reacting is that it allows you to think more clearly, making your reaction more productive.

This is true in any kind of conflict, but it's especially important to watch what we say to our partners. In a marriage, we often need to be vulnerable with each other. It's kind of like being emotionally naked. Words can hurt us more than if we were emotionally "clothed," or closed off. I would argue that the adage "Sticks and stones may break my bones, but words will never hurt me" gets it wrong, because unlike sticks and stones, words can stay with you forever. I'm sure I could ask you to recall the sweetest thing anyone has ever said to you and the meanest thing anyone has ever said to you, and you probably remember them both. That's how much power words have, so use them wisely.

MANAGE YOUR ANGER

Anger itself is not a sin—after all, even God Himself gets angry. Anger is a normal, acceptable emotion, just like any other. But anger can become a problem when we don't manage it properly. Managing anger is an essential life skill that we must master in our everyday lives as well as in our marriages. Strong emotions are naturally short-lived, but we often continue to "feed" them by stewing about the situation, constantly rehashing it and reliving it. Proverbs 29:11 tells us, "Fools give full vent to their rage, but the wise bring calm in the end." Here are some strategies to handle your anger wisely.

1. Talk it out! As long as you use an appropriate tone, you can say you're angry and explain why. Remember to use "I" statements rather than casting blame. "I feel .... when you ...."

2. Write about it. Use a journal or notebook to write out how you feel and why. If you're more of a doodler, you can draw instead. Usually getting the emotion out helps us feel better.

3. Exercise or dance. Moving vigorously helps calm the body down and produces endorphins, which improve your mood.

4. Practice deep breathing. It may sound clichéd, but taking deep breaths in and out helps calm you down by putting more oxygen into your body and slowing your heart rate.

5. Last, but certainly not least, pray about it. Ask God to help you manage your emotions, own your behavior, and grow as a person.

Be Straightforward but Compassionate

We should try to say what we mean and mean what we say at all times, but especially with our spouses. In chapter 2, I mentioned that many couples struggle to be assertive on challenging topics because they don't want to hurt their spouse's feelings or are afraid of how their spouse will react (see page 34). But it's impossible for your partner to meet your expectations if they don't even know what those expectations are.

Your needs are important, and they deserve to be heard, valued, and met. Just as you prioritize your spouse's needs, your spouse should prioritize yours. But neither of you can do that if you don't express to each other what your needs are, directly but kindly. So let it out, be honest and straightforward—but don't forget the compassion. *How* you say the words is as important as the words themselves. I joke with my clients that you could even tell your spouse they're ugly if you say it with compassion! It's all in the delivery. If your words are soft and gentle, you can talk honestly about even the thorniest subjects.

Here's an example of what I'm talking about. Let's say Kerlin comes home from a day at work and sees that Lisa has made a mess of the bedroom, throwing her dirty laundry everywhere. What should he say?

a. I'm sick of you treating me like the hired help! You don't appreciate all the hard work I put in!

b. (*heavy sigh*) No, I'm not mad, I'm fine. I'm just tired after a long day at work.

c. Honey, I love going to work each day and providing for our family. When I come home at the end of the day, I'm looking forward to relaxing and spending time with you. I know you don't mean it this way, but when I see you've left your dirty clothes all over the bedroom and I have to put them in the laundry basket, it makes me feel unappreciated and disrespected.

Option A is not compassionate enough. It will make Lisa feel defensive and will start a fight instead of a productive conversation. Option B is not straightforward enough. It may not start a fight now, but when Kerlin bottles up his frustration and Lisa doesn't understand why he's acting the way he is, it creates mutual discord and will lead to a fight later. Option C, on the other hand, is both straightforward and compassionate. It allows Lisa to hear what Kerlin has to say without feeling attacked and wanting to attack back.

HOW TO FIGHT FAIR

I've given you some strategies for stopping fights before they start, but sometimes fights are unavoidable. And that's okay! If you approach conflict from a place of love and respect, you can resolve it and make your relationship stronger in the process. Here are a few principles to keep in mind when you and your spouse are arguing.

Choose the Right Setting

Ensure the environment is conducive for a good dialogue. Don't try to fight it out during a party or in front of your kids. Do it in the comfort of your home, when it's just the two of you and you can focus on each other without distraction.

Let me give you an example. Lisa and Kerlin argued like cats and dogs in any environment they were in—at their friend's wedding, at the company holiday party, everywhere! They didn't care about the location. If they felt angry or frustrated, they'd display it. But over time, they began to see how this made everything worse. Both of them felt even more pressure to "win" because others were watching. Painful words became even more painful when they were used as a form of public embarrassment. Even worse, sometimes a third party would try to intervene or even take sides, which only heightened the conflict. Now they've learned that fighting in private makes it easier for them to stay calm, listen to each other, and eventually find a resolution.

Yelling Is Not Communication

All the honesty in the world won't help you fight fair if you start raising your voices and screaming at each other. You may think you're forcing your spouse to hear what you have to say, but in fact they are likely to get defensive, shut down, or scream right back at you. Remember the words of Ephesians 4:31: "Get rid of all bitterness, rage and anger, brawling and slander, along with every form of malice." We can only hear each other when we speak at a normal volume with words that allow us to listen with our hearts, not just our ears. If you find yourself struggling not to raise your voice, it's definitely time to take a time-out.

Take a Time-Out

Sometimes we get so worked up during fights that anything we say or do after a certain point is damaging to our relationship. When you find yourself in a situation where you're doing more harm than good, a time-out is in order. What's a time-out? It's a pause, a break from the situation (not the marriage). Think of it like a time-out in basketball. It doesn't end the game—it just allows the players to cool down, re-strategize, and come back with a winning plan. The same should apply to our marriages—except you and your spouse are on the same team.

As in basketball, your time-out should have rules. It should have an agreed-upon time limit, and when you return, you should be cooled down and focused on a plan for reunification. Too often, couples take the time-out, but then they use it to become more upset as they stew about what they should have said, the points they wish they'd made, all the wrongdoing they should have called out, and so on. The break should be a time for positive reflection, not negative deflection.

During a fight, we may be rigidly stuck on our own feelings and forget to consider the other person. It's natural to think about your own emotional safety. However, in marriage, you have a huge impact on your partner's emotional safety, not just your own. How do you show concern for your spouse's feelings? By valuing their perspective. Take a step back and consider what your partner feels, how they might view the situation, and what they might be thinking. This is empathy, the ability to share and understand someone else's feelings. Instead of thinking about what your spouse did wrong, think about how you could have responded better, how to correct the current situation, and what you need to do to improve the situation next time. Ask yourself questions like "How might my spouse have felt when I said that? How did it make me feel when we started to get heated? What was my spouse's body language?"

PLAN YOUR PAUSE

It's helpful to set rules for time-outs when you're *not* in the middle of a fight, so take a moment to write down the answers to these questions together. There's no right or wrong answer; the rules look different for every relationship.

1. What do we want our time-out to accomplish? (Be specific. Answers might include to calm down, to think of new strategies, or just to avoid saying mean things.)

2. If one of us feels the need for a time-out, how will we request it?

3. How long will the time-out last? (Typically 15 minutes to an hour works best.)

4. What will it look like when we reconnect? (Will you reconvene over a meal together to help calm your nerves? Will you sit on the floor face-to-face?)

5. Will we take the opportunity to apologize at the beginning of the reconnection?

6. Will we take the opportunity to use "I" statements about our emotions ("I felt .... when ....")?

AFTER THE FIGHT

Thank God for His grace and mercy! He is a merciful God who gives us second, fifth, and hundredth chances. In our efforts to be more like God, we must learn how to give grace and mercy to our spouses after a fight.

The first step is forgiveness. One of the reasons forgiveness is so hard sometimes is that it can feel like you're forgetting or excusing what happened. But forgiving someone doesn't mean that you're excusing sin. It means you recognize that we all make mistakes, which is why Jesus commands us to forgive so we will be forgiven (Luke 6:37). You forgive someone not because they didn't do anything wrong but to release your own anger and invite God's forgiveness into your own life. It's making the choice to give up the right to revenge in exchange for the right to love again. Just as you want God to forgive you, you must forgive others. Let's take a closer look at the concept of forgiveness and what to do in the aftermath of a fight.

Don't Hold a Grudge

Part of forgiveness is moving past the negative emotion that you felt during a conflict or other difficult situation. The reason you don't want to sit in anger for an extended period is because the longer you stew in it, the more accustomed you get to the pain. And the more accustomed to the pain you get, the more you hold on to it. That's the vicious cycle of holding a grudge.

Just imagine if God held grudges against us. What if you committed a sin in 2015, immediately repented, and then, when you asked God for something in 2020, He said, "Nope. Remember what you did to Me five years ago?" You would be devastated, right? Yet we do this to our spouses all too often.

Remember Proverbs 24:29: "Do not say, 'I'll do to them as they have done to me; I'll pay them back for what they did.'" When we try to pay back our spouses for something they did wrong, we're attempting to make ourselves feel better, but what we fail to realize is that we're preventing them from aiding in our own happiness. If you don't allow your spouse to make up for wrongdoing, you're not only harming your relationship, you're also leaving a void in your own heart. Grudges only hurt you and your marriage.

We're All Doing Our Best

People are not robots. We're people. We can't just push some buttons and program others to do what we want. For the most part, everyone is doing the best they know how. They're doing what they were taught or what they learned through their environment to be the correct way to behave. (That's the social learning theory we discussed in chapter 1 on page 2.) This doesn't excuse wrongdoing, but it reminds us to be patient, especially with our spouses.

Remember Lisa and Kerlin fighting about who paid what bills? Lisa grew up with a single mom who often told Lisa and her siblings that they had no say in what she decided for them because she was the one who paid all the bills. Kerlin grew up in a house where his dad made all the financial decisions and his mom never questioned it. Neither Lisa nor Kerlin ever saw a healthy discussion about money taking place when they were young, so they don't know how to handle it well and end up quarrelling about it constantly. But despite both their shortcomings, they're doing the best with the lives and lessons that have been given to them. They're slowly learning to give each other the benefit of the doubt. It may take them a while to get it, but they can learn to trust that the other is trying their best.

Remember that change takes time. It can be easy to feel like your spouse isn't listening, doesn't get it, or simply doesn't care, especially during a fight. But we all have the power to do better in the future. When we assume our spouse can't change, we forget that God can work on our spouse's heart. We assume the worst of our spouse (e.g., "He'll always be this way" or "She'll never change, so why bother trying?") instead of seeing the hope and grace that God gives us daily. So don't give up on your spouse.

CHRIST AS MEDIATOR

Hebrews 9:15 calls Christ "the mediator of a new covenant, that those who are called may receive the promised eternal inheritance." That new covenant means that we can be forgiven even when we sin. It's important to remember that and call on Jesus to help us follow His example when we find ourselves fighting with our partners. The next time you fight, try this guided prayer together as a couple:

Lord, please help us to bear the fruits of the spirit: love, joy, peace, forbearance, kindness, goodness, faithfulness, gentleness, and self-control. I know we have not been showing these fruits, Lord, but we want to do better. Please give us the strength to make these qualities daily habits. Help us become intentional in the way we treat each other and bring healing to our relationship. We ask You to be a part of our marriage and be our leader through this journey. We thank You for hearing our prayer, because we know we will have the marriage we desire through You. Amen.

Modeling Behavior

At some points in your marriage, you'll be following. At other times, you'll be leading. That's how a strong marriage ebbs and flows. One effective leadership strategy is modeling the behavior we want to see. Many of us understand this as it pertains to parenting, but we might not realize it applies to our behavior with our spouses or people in general as well.

It all comes back to what Jesus said in Luke 6:31: "Do to others as you would have them do to you." If you want your spouse to communicate more with you, communicate more with them. If you want more romance from your spouse, give more romance to them. If you want more forgiveness, be more forgiving. It's difficult to be intentionally negative toward someone who's being intentionally positive toward you. We can all learn from each other. Give the behavior you want to receive!

GIVE THANKS

Sometimes, in the midst of fighting and disagreements, we can begin to forget how much we love our spouses most of the time. We might feel like certain challenges are *always* happening, when really they're only happening *right now*. But remember, instead of dwelling on the negative, we can redirect our thoughts to the gratitude we feel for our spouses, our families, and everything else God has given us. Here's an exercise to help you remember to give thanks every day.

In the morning: Start each day by telling God what you're grateful for, and leave a short, simple note of gratitude somewhere in the house for your family. For example, write it on a sticky note and put it on the refrigerator so your household can see what you're thankful for. (This has the added benefit of modeling gratitude.)

At night: Before bed, listen to a song that reminds you of God's goodness, and let that song lead you into your nightly prayer, beginning with thanksgiving.

Try doing both of these things every day for at least a week. You might keep it going for longer once you see the effect it has!

COMMITTED ACTION

Arguments can really damage a marriage, but if you fight fair, you can learn to resolve conflicts and actually make your relationship stronger. Here are a few things I want to make sure you take away and apply to your marriage right away!

1. Be "quick to listen and slow to speak," as James 1:19 says. Most of our arguments come from miscommunication. Most miscommunication arises when we listen to respond rather than to understand.

2. Remember, it's perfectly normal to feel angry sometimes, but you don't want to live there. You can learn to manage your anger so that it doesn't rule your behavior and poison your relationship with your spouse.

3. Don't forget forgiveness. Forgiveness gives you, your spouse, and your marriage another chance. Forgiving others isn't just for them. It's also for God and even for you!

Let him kiss me with the kisses of his mouth—for your love is more delightful than wine . . . Take me away with you—let us hurry! Let the king bring me into his chambers.

Song of Songs 1:1-4

CHAPTER FOUR

INTIMACY

THE WORD "INTIMACY" CAN MEAN MANY things, from emotional closeness to sex. It can be scary to be vulnerable with another person, but the rewards are worth it. This chapter will guide you through intimacy in all its forms and help you start tackling intimacy issues.

DEFINING INTIMACY

Intimacy doesn't just refer to sex. There are actually five different types of intimacy—emotional, physical, intellectual, experiential, and spiritual—that are all necessary for your marriage in different ways.

Emotional Intimacy

Emotional intimacy is defined by the ability to share our feelings and innermost selves with each other openly and honestly. It's what bonds a couple together and gives them a sense of closeness. It is the foundation of all forms of intimacy, though because it's less concrete than the others, it can be trickier to understand and navigate. Emotional intimacy is being able to share your deepest, darkest fears with your spouse and trust that they won't laugh at you or judge you. Emotional intimacy is being able to walk into a room and know exactly how your spouse is feeling just because you know their face and body language so well. So much of this goes unspoken, but it is the basis of love, connection, care, and closeness.

Physical Intimacy

Physical intimacy is closeness that involves the body. This includes sex, but it also includes hugging, kissing, cuddling, holding hands, and even deep eye contact. Nonsexual touch creates the foundation of physical intimacy, and sexual intercourse builds on it. While some people treat it like it's not as important as emotional intimacy, I tell my couples that physical intimacy can and will bring you closer and help you connect with each other on an emotional level. I encourage all my clients to engage in healthy sexual intimacy as often as possible. Sex is as necessary to a marriage as sun and water are to a flower. It helps us grow closer and stay connected.

On the topic of sex, 1 Corinthians 7:3 tells us, "The husband should fulfill his marital duty to his wife, and likewise the wife to her husband." This shows us the importance of sexual intimacy in marriage, but we must be careful not to take it out of context and interpret it to mean that one spouse should be able to force the other into doing things they don't want to do. It is, of course, true that we should freely give physical intimacy to our spouses, and we shouldn't intentionally withhold sex as an act of revenge. But remember that we are human beings with our own needs, wants, and limitations. There is no one-size-fits-all rule about sex, and I remind my couples that there are always exceptions and times when we'll need to be patient with each other. Therefore, yes, please enjoy the sexual intimacy that God made for marriage. But also be mindful of your spouse's physical and mental health, and be patient as intimacy ebbs and flows.

Intellectual Intimacy

Intellectual intimacy is a brain-to-brain connection, but it has nothing to do with IQ or intelligence. Rather, it's about your ability to communicate across the topic spectrum and be considerate with each other while doing so. It's what you do when you and your spouse discuss the movie you just saw together or what you both think about a political issue, and you're both interested to hear what the other has to say. With strong intellectual intimacy, couples can have in-depth conversations on spirituality, sex, finances, politics, and everything in between—and remain comfortable or even excited while they do.

Experiential Intimacy

Experiential intimacy is found in the joy of shared activities. It's the intimacy that develops through activities together such as joining a bowling league, painting, or taking ballroom dance classes. Often, experiential intimacy jump-starts a relationship as newly dating couples make an effort to do fun things together, but it falls off as they become more comfortable with each other. We see many married couples in our office who have stopped going on dates altogether. Why? To sum it up: life! When we have to deal with jobs, kids, bills, health challenges, and so on, the first place we cut back is our leisure time, and that's where most of our experiential intimacy is stored.

Spiritual Intimacy

Spiritual intimacy is a sense of unity and mutual commitment to God's purpose for our lives and marriages, along with a respect for the special dreams of each other's hearts. This might look like sharing your prayers or your thoughts about faith with each other, studying the Bible together, or volunteering at church together. In order to develop spiritual intimacy with your spouse, you must first have intimacy between yourself and God.

We must remember that in a godly marriage, there are three relationships: (1) the relationship between the two spouses, (2) the relationship between each individual spouse and God, and (3) the spouses' mutual relationship with God. We must get to know God for ourselves by talking to Him through prayer, listening to His Word, serving Him through ministry, and so on. If you're emotionally intimate with each other and both spiritually intimate with God, then you can share spiritual intimacy with each other.

UNDERSTANDING THE VALUE OF INTIMACY

Now that you know what the five main forms of intimacy are, let's discuss the value they bring to your marriage.

1. Intimacy brings you closer. The connection you make through intimacy is like no other. You can help this closeness grow by giving your undivided attention to your spouse and truly focusing on each other without distractions.

2. Intimacy allows you to become more selfless. When you fill your spouse's intimacy bucket, your intent should be to overflow them with your love, like the cup that "runneth over" in Psalm 23:5 (KJV). They're doing the same with you, so as you meet your spouse's needs, you also meet your own needs in a beautiful cycle of give and take. With deep intimacy, you stop fearing that your needs will go unmet and therefore don't feel the need to act selfishly or defensively.

3. Intimacy builds trust. For better or worse, your childhood years are when you learned about trust. If your parental figures broke promises, neglected or abandoned you in some capacity, or were abusive, it probably caused you to see the world with distrust. But even if you start from a very suspicious place, building intimacy with your spouse will help you build trust, which will help you build more intimacy, and so forth.

Interdependence, not Codependence

Chapter 1 of this book was about "leaving and cleaving," a concept found in Genesis 2:24: "That is why a man leaves his father and mother and is united to his wife, and they become one flesh." It's easy to take this scripture out of context. Intimacy lets us unite with each other as Genesis describes, but becoming one flesh doesn't mean you should suffocate each other, spending every waking moment together and always agreeing on everything. If you did, you'd probably become codependent.

In a codependent relationship, one person relies on the other to meet nearly all their emotional and self-esteem needs—and the person being relied upon will go to any lengths to keep their partner happy, even when it enables dysfunctional behavior. One classic example of codependency is when one partner is an alcoholic, and instead of helping them to get the professional assistance they need, the other partner helps keep them "happy" by supplying more alcohol, smoothing over any conflicts that happen with others as a result of the alcoholism, and so on. This is a dangerous dynamic for anyone. We are all ultimately responsible for our own happiness and our own behavior. Our spouses enhance our lives, not create them.

Instead of fostering codependency, healthy intimacy helps build interdependency. An interdependent relationship is one in which each partner is their own individual, but they play as a team in order to win at life. They're aware of their individual responsibilities, but they can pick up slack for each other if needed. They lean on each other for support, but they can also accomplish things on their own, and they don't enable each other to keep engaging in harmful behavior. It's a relationship that allows for weakness *and* strength, needing help *and* helping.

Which brings me to another verse I love from Genesis: "The Lord God said, 'It is not good for the man to be alone. I will make a helper suitable for him'" (2:18). Some people interpret this to mean that the wife in a marriage has an inferior position, but as a wife, I love being a helper. Being a helper doesn't mean that you're weak; it's actually quite the opposite. If I'm struggling with college-level math, I'm not going to seek help from a second grader who knows nothing about it. To the contrary, I would want someone extremely skilled to help me—my professor or someone else who specializes in math. If God considers wives to be helpers to their husbands, then He holds them in very high regard. And there's nothing that says the help can't be mutual. With true intimacy, it goes both ways.

HANDLING INTIMACY ISSUES

Money may be the most common thing couples fight about, but sex isn't far behind. One of the challenges I often see with my Christian couples is the transition from practicing abstinence to being a married couple taking on new sexual identities and pressures. For a lot of people, it's challenging to avoid sex your entire life and then suddenly switch to trying to achieve sexual satisfaction. Many couples are fearful and uneducated due to lack of experience. Expecting them—or any couple, really—to build a healthy sex life without a strong support system is like asking fourth graders to pass a trigonometry exam. Well, guess what? This book is your study guide, and you're about to learn some trigonometry, no matter how experienced or inexperienced you may be.

BIBLE STUDY: SONG OF SONGS

Song of Songs, also known as Song of Solomon, is a lyrical poem about love and intimacy—yes, that includes sexual intimacy. Take some time to read the entire book with your spouse (it's only a few pages long) and then answer the following questions in your journal or notebook.

1. When was the last time you felt joy like the couple in Song of Songs?
2. Does it feel unfamiliar to think of biblical sex as joyful?
3. What parts did you find the most beautiful?
4. What parts did you find the most surprising?
5. Many say Songs is a sexual guide for couples. What do you think about that?

Don't Take It Personally

Couples who communicate about their intimacy have a stronger sexual connection, but for many people these conversations can be nerve-racking. They avoid these conversations and keep sweeping the problem under the rug—or, I should say, they *think* they're sweeping the problem under the rug, when in fact they're only letting it grow bigger and bigger.

One of the reasons sex is such a sensitive topic is that it's very easy to take these conversations personally and mistakenly assume that because your partner is dissatisfied with your sex life in some way, they must be dissatisfied with you as a spouse or as a person. One spouse could say something as simple as, "I would like our sex life to be more spontaneous," and the other spouse might take it to mean that they're no longer attractive or lovable. Couples are afraid of that possibility, so they often avoid the conversation altogether. We have to learn to approach intimacy issues with the assurance that no one is under attack; you're just addressing your sex life together in order to find a solution that works for everyone.

As with any serious conversation, you want to communicate with a mix of assertiveness and compassion, using "I" statements to discuss how you feel without blaming your spouse.

Unhelpful: *You never want to have sex anymore. You reject me every time I bring it up.*

Helpful: *I feel rejected when I try to cuddle with you and you tell me to get off you.*

The second version allows you to own your feelings without accusing your spouse of rejecting you.

If you're the spouse receiving this information, you're the active listener, which means you need to listen with your heart and not just with your ears. Reflect on your partner's words and ensure you completely understand their emotion before you give your response. When you both trust each other to listen to, understand, and accept each other's feelings, desires, and needs, it lets you build intimacy, both emotional and physical.

Consider Past Experiences

One reason sexual intimacy can be difficult for couples is due to baggage from previous relationships, trauma due to sexual assault, or both. This is a good place for me to use an example based on a situation I've seen many times.

Mei and Benjamin were having intimacy issues. Mei had previously been married to someone else for five years. The marriage had been unhealthy in many ways, one of which was their sex life. Her previous husband spoke to her about sex in a degrading way, and often used God's Word to pressure her into sexual acts she didn't want. Ultimately, she divorced him and later married Benjamin. But, as you can imagine, Mei had a lot of baggage from her first marriage. She didn't trust Benjamin with her body, because her trust had been violated so deeply by her first husband. On top of that, it was hard for her to seek comfort in scripture, because her first husband had misused it to control her. Mei needed a lot of support, patience, and couples therapy to get to a place where she could have a healthy sex life with Benjamin.

Baggage can also work in the opposite way. If you were previously married and had a good sex life, it can be difficult to readjust to a sex life with someone new. Whatever a person's sexual past may be, it's important to remember that it will have an effect on their present.

Be Patient

Proverbs 25:15 reminds us that "through patience a ruler can be persuaded, and a gentle tongue can break a bone." Whatever intimacy issues you're facing, they won't get fixed overnight. Trying to force a conversation won't help (and, it goes without saying, trying to pressure someone into a sexual act is always wrong). Instead, lead your spouse into positive conversations using the tools in this book, and demonstrate patience with the process. It will help your spouse trust you more—which, as we know, is the basis of true intimacy.

SEX TALK GROUND RULES

Talking about sex can be intimidating at first, but face it head-on and your bravery will pay off. Here are a few ground rules to get you started.

1. Intimacy is based on trust. Build trust by not blind-siding your spouse with the topic of sex. Let them know you want to talk with them about improving your sex life in advance of the conversation. Give them time to think about the topic and what areas they may want to discuss.

2. Choose the appropriate time to have a conversation, not when you're busy with other things and not in bed. (Even if you're just getting ready to sleep, one person might begin to yawn or drift off, coming across as unengaged when really they're just sleepy.) Definitely don't try to bring it up in the middle of other hot topics like money or co-parenting.

3. During the conversation, don't pressure each other to answer in a certain way. Truly listen and respect the dialogue between you on the topic.

REKINDLING ROMANCE

What causes a couple to go from hot and steamy to boring roommates? Sometimes it's as simple as getting busy with life and slipping into a sexless routine. Sometimes external forces have an effect. Chip and Kristy, for example, had always been proud of their sex life. They had three children and demanding careers in the banking industry, but after 10 years of marriage, they were still going strong. But all that changed when Chip was laid off. It was a huge financial setback for the couple, as they had created a lifestyle based on two hardy incomes. They had to pull their kids from private school and cut back on many of the amenities they had grown accustomed to. The stress of this situation put a strain on their marriage in more ways than one. Before they knew it, all Chip and Kristy did was argue and stress over money problems, which ultimately drained their intimacy. They found themselves in a rut and were barely touching each other.

If this scenario sounds familiar to you, it's time to rekindle the romance and bring the steaminess back! And to do that, you'll have to be intentional with your actions and words.

The Little Things

Marriage is one big thing made up of a thousand little things that require sacrifice, patience, and selflessness. Actually, my favorite part of working with couples is educating them on all the small things that make marriage work! So many times we get caught up in thinking we have to make grand romantic gestures with extravagant gifts or elaborate events, but in reality, nothing could be further from the truth. In the happiest marriages you'll find two people whose small actions build up to a big love.

Try a few of these little things to remind your partner you care and help rekindle your romance:

- Bring home their favorite candy bar.
- Open their car door for them.
- Kiss the back of their neck while they're cooking.
- Wash the dishes on a night when it's not your turn.
- Bring a cup of cold water to them while they're doing yardwork.
- Give them a compliment before they leave for work in the morning.
- Rest your hand on their leg when you're sitting together.
- Fix their plate for them at dinnertime.

Ask Questions

Between careers, growing older, children, and social lives, our likes and dislikes shift throughout our lives. The things that excited us 10 years ago may be boring now, and we may now be interested in things we'd never heard of when we were young. Relationship researcher John Gottman teaches that there are three steps to mutual understanding: (1) asking questions, (2) remembering the answers, and (3) asking more questions.

We often assume that we know everything about our spouses because we've been together so long. But people grow and change. We want to grow along with our spouses, not grow apart from them. By practicing the three parts of mutual understanding, we can stay emotionally intimate with our spouses, learning what we don't know and what's brand new. When we talk about sex and romance in this way, it helps us maintain physical intimacy as well.

If you do have conversations about your sexual desires but still feel unfulfilled, you might need to pay more attention to step 2: remembering the answers. Sometimes we talk about what we want but don't actually take it to heart and apply it. Remembering your spouse's wishes for romance is the difference between staying steamy and becoming romantically depleted. Pay attention. You can even take notes! Yes, it's okay to write down your spouse's words—that way you can reflect back on them often.

GETTING TO KNOW YOU (AGAIN)

Want some conversation starters to help you reignite your romantic life? Try asking each other these questions, and write down each other's answers in your journal or notebook. Then remember those answers—and ask more questions!

- How do you define romance?
- What would be an ideal romantic date?
- What are three romantic things I can say to you verbally?
- What are three romantic actions I can do for you?
- What are three romantic places I could take you?

Remember that the little things are just as important as the big things, so feel free to describe scents, foods, holding hands, and so on.

DON'T WITHHOLD INTIMACY

There are a million different reasons why couples don't have as much sex as they'd like to, but one particularly egregious one is deliberately withholding intimacy as a form of revenge. I see more and more couples doing this, and I don't think God is pleased with it. The Bible tells us that "Love is patient, love is kind. It does not envy, it does not boast, it is not proud. It does not dishonor others, it is not self-seeking, it is not easily angered, it keeps no record of wrongs" (1 Corinthians 13:4–5). If love is everything described above and we are to love our spouses as Christ loves the church (Ephesians 5:25), then you can see how intentionally withholding intimacy is not pleasing to God.

To be clear, if one spouse has a lower libido and doesn't want to have sex as often, that doesn't count as deliberately withholding sex. Nor is it withholding sex if you're, say, angry at your spouse and therefore don't really feel in the mood. And even if your spouse *is* withholding sex, you never have the right to force them into anything.

But what I'm saying is that if you reach the point where your intimacy as a couple is so broken that one of you is unilaterally shutting down all forms of sexual intimacy, then you are no longer operating as a team or loving each other as God commands. Instead of cutting your spouse off, talk through your emotions to get back on the same page and continue to love. (Note that this doesn't apply in cases of infidelity and abuse, which we'll discuss in greater detail in chapter 6.)

TAKING ACTION TO RESTORE INTIMACY

We've discussed a lot of the big and sometimes intimidating concepts around intimacy issues like communication, patience, and biblical principles. But there are some pretty simple actions you can take to improve the situation as well.

One action is scheduling sex. Yes—scheduling sex! If you can't find time for spontaneous sex, then make time for non-spontaneous sex. It may not seem as romantic or hot at first, but being intentional about sex lets you reestablish the physical intimacy you need for your marriage to thrive. And who knows? Once you get back in the swing of it, you may not need to schedule it anymore.

Another action is actively paying attention to what turns your spouse on and doing those things. If you know your spouse gets excited when you touch their lower back, use that as a tool to aid in restoring intimacy. Do the things that make your spouse feel sexual.

These kinds of simple actions don't just help initiate physical intimacy in the moment—they also help develop a consistent pattern of intimacy that can only benefit your relationship.

CHANGE THE NARRATIVE

Sometimes we get stuck in a rut where we're not having sex or even holding hands. We have our reasons, but instead of working to change those reasons, we become attached to them as excuses. It's time to change the narrative!

Take a sheet of paper and draw a vertical line down the middle. In the left-hand column, write down all the excuses you've become used to using. On the right side, work together to come up with a remedy for each excuse listed. For example:

• We don't have time for sex.	• We can cut something out of our schedules to make time for sex.
• We work opposite schedules.	• We can schedule sex ahead of time for when we're both home.
• Our kids always get in the way.	• We can put on a movie for the kids to watch while we have date night.

When you're done, start putting those remedies into action!

COMMITTED ACTION

We went over many facets of intimacy in this chapter, but there are a few things I want to highlight so you can start enacting them right away.

1. There are five main forms of intimacy: emotional, physical, intellectual, experiential, and spiritual. Emotional intimacy is the basis for all the others. Schedule some time with your spouse to go through each of the five forms and give yourselves a grade. Which ones are you doing well in and which need more growth?

2. Accept the challenge and talk about intimacy without fear! Communicate with assertiveness and compassion using "I" statements, and don't take healthy discussion of your sex life as a personal insult or rejection.

3. Exercise your most important sexual organ: your brain! Talking and doing activities together increases all forms of intimacy between you and your spouse. And remember to use that big brain of yours to ask your partner questions, remember the answers, and then ask more questions.

*Any kingdom divided against itself
will be ruined, and a house
divided against itself will fall.*

Luke 11:17

CHAPTER FIVE

TEAM UP

MARRIAGE IS A TEAM SPORT. Though it might sometimes feel like you and your spouse are going head-to-head, you're actually teammates. You're not playing *against* each other. You're working *with* each other to win. This chapter is all about how to share responsibilities, challenges, and victories as members of the same team.

TEAMWORK

The Bible is very clear about why operating as a team beats working solo. Ecclesiastes 4:9–10 tells us, "Two are better than one, because they have a good return for their labor; if either of them falls down, one can help the other up. But pity anyone who falls and has no one to help them up." My favorite part is in verse 12, when God includes Himself on our team: "A cord of three strands is not quickly broken." We can see that teamwork is helpful or even necessary in nearly every situation. We are uniquely and divinely made individuals who, when we come together, create a mighty force!

Let's take a closer look at what teamwork means in marriage.

The Sanctuary of Marriage

When I first got married, my elders suggested that I create a home that would be peaceful for my husband. I remember asking, "What does that mean exactly?" They responded that home should be a place where he could be heard, feel safe, relax, and be comforted. That was many years ago, and now that I've lived out marriage myself, I wholeheartedly agree with that sentiment—except that it was missing one thing: reciprocity. Both spouses are members of the same team, so both should create a sanctuary for the other. God wants us to be each other's refuge, retreat, and security.

Maintaining our faith in God is the foundation of creating a sanctuary in marriage. The more we learn to keep God and his commandments first, the more we learn to love each other as God loves the church. As we think about treating others as God treats us, then learning to be each other's sanctuary is easier to understand. Psalm 9:9 says, "The Lord is a refuge for the oppressed, a stronghold in times of trouble." We need to be intentional in ensuring that assertiveness with compassion, active listening, forgiveness, kindness, and love define our sanctuaries.

Give Your Spouse a Break

Common marriage vows often include the phrase "in sickness and in health." Sometimes the "sickness" can simply be reaching a point where you're feeling sick of each other or overwhelmed by life. These things lead to breakdowns in other areas of your relationship. Usually (but not always), the first thing to crumble under stress is a couple's communication with each other, followed by their sex life, and then everything else. In order to prevent things from reaching this point, it's important to remember to be understanding and give each other a break when necessary.

Here's an example of what I'm talking about. Lorenzo and Elienna have been under a lot of stress lately. Both of them work full-time at demanding jobs, and one of Lorenzo's coworkers recently left the company, meaning he's had to take over a lot of additional responsibilities on top of his own. Meanwhile, one of their three kids was recently diagnosed with a learning disability, and Elienna has taken on most of the work of communicating with doctors, therapists, and teachers to make sure their child gets the right education plan. Both have parents who are getting older and increasingly need more support navigating the demands of daily life like shopping and cooking. With all these competing demands, it can be hard for them to remember they're on a team together.

ELIENNA: *Honey, I thought you said you were going to make dinner tonight.*

LORENZO: *I know, but I just couldn't do it today. I've been so busy with work, and the kids are driving me crazy! All I want to do is sit down and relax in front of the TV for a while.*

ELIENNA: *That's all you want to do lately! Lay around and not help out around the house! Do I have to do everything around here? Don't you even care about this family?*

LORENZO: *Are you serious? With the hours I work to keep a roof over our heads? Meanwhile the dishes are piling up in the sink because you're too lazy to do them.*

In this scenario, Elienna and Lorenzo saw each other as adversaries competing over who would do the task that neither one of them wanted to do (make dinner). They were looking out for their own individual interests rather than their interests as a team. What if they gave each other a break instead?

ELIENNA: *Honey, I thought you said you were going to make dinner tonight.*

LORENZO: *I know, I meant to, but I just couldn't do it today. With all the extra work I'm doing to make up for Terry leaving, I'm so exhausted after work.*

ELIENNA: *I wish you'd told me earlier, but I understand how hard you're working right now. Why don't we just order a pizza tonight?*

LORENZO: *I'm sorry for not communicating earlier. I know you're working extra hard right now too. Pizza sounds great.*

In the second scenario, instead of focusing on their own desires, Lorenzo and Elienna kept their focus on their mutual goal of getting dinner on the table for their family. Instead of demanding perfection from each other, they demonstrated understanding and leniency.

Serving Your Partner

Service is an essential part of marriage and was designed that way by God. God serves us (through His care, love, and mercy for us), and in return, we serve God (through our everyday lives and our relationships with Him). This is exactly how we are to serve our spouses and in return be served by them. Yes, this might mean "taking one for the team" or handling something individually if your partner is unable or unwilling, but it also means serving each other in Christ's name and modeling positive behavior for each other.

Pastor and writer Jimmy Evans breaks this down beautifully by making the word "serve" an acronym.

- **Supply** what your spouse needs in spite of what you need, want, or understand.
- **Enjoy** serving your spouse and do it with a joyful attitude.
- **Reject** scorekeeping.
- **Vigilantly** protect the priority of your marriage.
- **Expect** to be blessed.

I absolutely love this perspective! It encourages selfless-ness and giving with a positive attitude and then seals it with God's promise that if we live for Him, He will give us the desires of our heart—*if* we learn the art of serving others.

MUTUAL SERVICE: THE BIBLICAL VIEW

One piece of scripture that comes up a lot in discus-sions about Christian marriages is in Ephesians 5. It starts off, "Wives, submit yourselves to your own hus-bands as you do to the Lord. For the husband is the head of the wife as Christ is the head of the church" (5:22–23). Many people think this means women are "less than" in a marriage, and that their purpose is to serve their husbands.

But let's look at verse 25: "Husbands, love your wives, just as Christ loved the church and gave himself up for her to make her holy." And how did Christ show his love for the church? According to Mark 10:45, "the Son of Man did not come to be served, but to serve, and to give his life as a ransom for many." So, yes, wives are supposed to serve their husbands—but husbands are also supposed to serve their wives, just like Jesus.

Ephesians 5:30–31 concludes by saying that hus-band and wife are "one flesh" (there's that leaving and cleaving again!) just as members of the church are all members of Christ's body. In marriage, neither partner is "less than" the other. You are both part of the same body and the same team.

ROLES IN MARRIAGE

In marriage, you and your spouse both play roles that contribute to the overall well-being of the union. Every marriage divides up these roles differently. Some couples practice traditional gender-specific roles, while others choose roles based on the individuals' strengths, weaknesses, and interests. Couples often switch back and forth between roles depending on time and availability. Any of these methods can be valid. The crucial thing is that you're both content with your roles, and that if someone isn't content, you stay open to conversations about roles changing and evolving. Our roles should be satisfactory to us as individuals, but they should also keep our families functioning so that both we and our spouses get our needs met.

Flexibility

Let's go back to the analogy of team sports for a moment. In basketball, every player on the team has a role. You have a point guard, a shooting guard, a small forward, a power forward, and a center on the court at all times. Each player has their own individual responsibilities, but each can play offense or defense as the situation calls for it, and each can shoot the ball. The teammates who aren't currently on the court have the role of cheering on and supporting those who are—but at any moment, someone on the bench could be put in the game and those roles could switch. The players have to be flexible and understand that their ultimate goal is to win together. Their roles may change, but they're still part of the same team.

Marriage is no different! Maybe at the beginning of your marriage, you're managing the finances, but one year later, you realize you're struggling to ensure that the bills are paid in a timely manner. This may be an opportunity for you and your spouse to reexamine your roles. Maybe your partner could take over paying the bills and you could take on one of their roles in return, or you could keep paying some bills while your partner takes over paying others.

Let's recall Ecclesiastes 3: "There is a time for everything, and a season for every activity under the heavens . . . a time to tear down and a time to build, a time to weep and a time to laugh, a time to mourn and a time to dance." Different seasons in life may call for different roles. The important thing is to be clear which role you're playing and what that looks like, yet stay flexible enough to do whatever is necessary for your team to win, even if it's not your "traditional" role.

Picking Up Slack

In many ways, we're the busiest we've ever been. Many of you reading this are managing multiple facets of life at once: marriage, career, children (and everything they have going on), household chores, volunteer positions in church and/ or civic groups, home improvement projects, hobbies, and so on. When you're juggling that many balls, it becomes easier to drop one.

So be vigilant and pay attention to your spouse. Are they struggling to get everything done? What are their energy levels like? If your spouse is slipping and it affects your life, your first instinct may be to criticize. Instead, turn that into an urge to support and pick up slack in the areas where your spouse may be dropping the ball. After all, it's our responsibility to be helpmeets for our spouses! If your spouse normally mows the lawn every Saturday but didn't find time to do it this week, you can offer to do it for them, or just agree that it's fine to leave it until next week.

Change Your Perspective

Sometimes we can become bitter or resentful about supporting a spouse, especially if we've recently been picking up slack for them or if we feel they're not reciprocating. You can work on that by changing your perspective. Instead of viewing helping your spouse as a duty or obligation, think of it as a responsibility or an opportunity. God tells us to give "not reluctantly or under compulsion" but rather to be "a cheerful giver" (2 Corinthians 9:7). Give your help from a spirit of shared responsibility, not a sense of grudging duty.

Ivan, for example, sees it as a chore to help his wife Michelle with the cooking. He actually enjoys making certain dishes, but he only wants to do it when he feels like it, because he believes that it's a woman's duty to cook, and he doesn't have much flexibility in his beliefs. Michelle has communicated to Ivan that providing food for their family is a duty they both share, but that hasn't done much to convince him. One day, Michelle decided to try presenting it to him differently. She started talking about Ivan cooking as an opportunity to be a teammate, and the team's goal was to eat. Over time, this helped change Ivan's heart. Although they still have some arguments about it, Ivan now does a better job of sharing the responsibility of cooking for the family.

MANAGING MONEY AS A TEAM

As I've mentioned—and as you likely know firsthand—finances can cause a lot of conflict for couples. This topic can be the source of so much strife that many people believe that money is the root of all evil. But the Bible actually says it's the *love* of money that's the root of evil (1 Timothy 6:10). You shouldn't be more focused on money than you are on God or on your family, but you still have to deal with it every day. If couples don't master teamwork around money, then it will inevitably become a thorn in their side. There are many philosophies and theories about the best ways to save and spend money, but that won't be my focus in this section.

Rather, I'm going to talk about how to manage money as a team.

Communicating about Money as a Team

The first step in learning to deal with money as a team is learning to talk about it as a team. I frequently see money conversations get heated when couples begin speaking from an individual perspective rather than a mutual perspective. They talk about "my money," "my spending," "my investments," not "our money," "our spending," "our investments." Believe it or not, words have power, so if you talk about your finances as if you're not a team, you'll likely make decisions about your money as if you're not a team.

Sometimes we get so stuck in our own perspective that we're not even sure what a conversation about finances could look like from any other point of view. Many couples ask me, "When we have a conversation about money, what are we supposed to talk about?" Here are some issues I think it's important to communicate about. If you can engage in healthy conversations on these topics, you're well on your way to financial teamwork.

- Should you have individual bank accounts, shared bank accounts, or a combination of both?
- How will you handle paying bills? If you're both earning income, will both incomes be used for all bills, or will one of you fund some bills while the other funds others? Will one of you manage the act of paying the bills (via check or online), or will you split that responsibility up?
- What are your views on debt? What level of debt do you have, individually and/or as a couple? Do you and your

spouse have a debt plan? If so, is it currently working? If not, how can you learn to create one that does? Does debt reduction come from your regular income, or do you have a special account set aside?

- What are your views on investing? If you invest, do you do so separately or together? What do you do with the income from investments?
- Do you have financial goals? If so, what are they? If not, how can you set some, and what should they be?

If it's helpful, you can each write down your thoughts on these questions in your own journal or notebook before sharing with each other. If the conversation becomes heated, take a break and revisit what you learned about fighting fair in chapter 3 (see page 60).

Make a Budget

The Bible tells us that "where there is no vision, the people perish" (Proverbs 29:18, KJV). Within your marriage, you and your spouse are the visionaries for your family. It's important to have a plan and stick to it as much as possible in order to reach the goals you've set as a family. I often hear couples say, "We don't have enough money to make a budget," or, conversely, "We have great income, so we don't need to make a budget." Both of these statements are incorrect. Having a plan and a budget isn't based on the amount of income you have, it's based on how you want to manage what you have, whether that's $1,000 or $100,000. Your budget should take into account your income, regular household expenses, leisure allowance, savings, and so on. (And when you talk about savings, discuss not just what you want to save but also what you're saving it for.)

José and Katrina are working on their budget right now. They've had some disagreements about savings, because Katrina wants to save every spare dime while José understands the importance of saving for the future but also wants to live comfortably in the present. Here's a productive conversation they had on this subject.

KATRINA: *I'm so excited we're saving money now. I want to get out of debt as soon as possible.*

JOSÉ: *Me too! I'm glad we've agreed on an amount to save each month after paying our bills. Now I can drop a few dollars into savings and then have a few dollars to spend for myself.*

KATRINA: *But if you have a few dollars left over, don't you think they should go into savings? Then you can get out of debt faster.*

JOSÉ: *I think that since we're staying on track with our savings plan, we should be able to enjoy some leisure funds as well. It helps me feel like I'm living for today while still preparing for tomorrow.*

KATRINA: *Hm, okay, I understand that. Maybe I'll do that, too. I have been wanting to invest in a membership to that new gym!*

Be Open and Honest

Nothing that we've discussed so far will work without honesty and openness. Could you imagine trying to create a plan or budget without knowing how much money you're actually working with or how much debt you actually have? Planning would be a waste of time, and it'd probably be frustrating to feel like you're spinning your wheels. It's critical to speak with truth about your debt, spending habits, financial fears, financial needs, bills that are causing you stress, and so on. Only in this most truthful space can you create and manage a real plan as a team.

Allow me to show you two examples with very different outcomes.

TOM: *Honey, don't forget that we agreed to bring our pay stubs to the kitchen table for our money meeting this evening.*

LINDSEY: *You know, I've been thinking about it, and I think you should just tell me how much I need to transfer to the bill-paying account. You don't need to know how much my paycheck is. I mean, I'm the one who works for it, not you. And as long as I pay my fair share, then it shouldn't be a problem.*

Lindsey might be right that the bills will get paid as long as she pays her fair share, but she's certainly not managing money as a team player. Here's a different way the same conversation could've played out.

TOM: *Honey, don't forget that we agreed to bring our pay stubs to the kitchen table for our money meeting this evening.*

LINDSEY: *I've been thinking about that conversation all day. I'm nervous about it because I've never shared my pay stub with anyone. I've worked so hard to get where I am with my career and I have this fear that someone will take it away from me. I'm going to need your patience through this process as I learn to get over this fear.*

In this version of the conversation, Lindsey has the same insecurities, but she's working toward trusting Tom and managing their money together as a team.

BIBLE STUDY: GENEROSITY

If you lend money to one of my people among you who is needy, do not treat it like a business deal; charge not interest. If you take your neighbor's cloak as a pledge, return it by sunset, because that cloak is the only covering your neighbor has.

Exodus 22:25-27

Answer these questions in your journal or notebook, then discuss with your spouse.

- Who do you think this scripture is intended for?
- How does this apply to your finances as a couple?
- What do you think the Bible is saying about giving?
- What do you think the Bible is saying about receiving?

A FAMILY AFFAIR

The most basic definition of family is a group of people who share a bond either genetically or legally. But that's a very simple sentence for such a monumental word. Whether you're parenting children who still live at home, assisting adult children, helping raise grandchildren, or caring for your parents in their old age, we're all part of a family in some shape, form, or fashion. As 1 Timothy 5:8 says, "Anyone who does not provide for their relatives, and especially for their own household, has denied the faith," so family is an important part of any conversation on teamwork in your marriage. No one can deny how much work it is to be part of a family, especially an extended family, but in the end, it's well worth the effort and patience.

Precious Gifts

Children and family are gifts from God. My proudest memories are of the days I gave birth to my children. The Bible tells us that children are a blessing. There are many times when Jesus took children into His hands to heal them or pray for them, which signifies how important children were to Him—and, by extension, how important they should be to us as well.

I love what Luke 18:15–17 teaches us. When people brought babies for Jesus to bless, His disciples tried to turn them away. "But Jesus called the children to him and said, 'Let the little children come to me, and do not hinder them, for the kingdom of God belongs to such as these.'" This scripture reminds us how to care for our children: to encourage them to come to us, be held by us, be cared for and loved by us! The Bible also tells us God will be "a father to the fatherless" (Psalm 68:5). I'm always in awe of the birthing process that God designed, but I also understand that your family is who He gives you to care for, which may include people you didn't give birth to or who aren't even related to you by blood. Family is the fundamental institution of human society.

Parenting as a Team

As the mother of three children, I cannot emphasize enough the importance of being on the same page when it comes to parenting. I always tell my couples that you should be a united front when it comes to parenting, because our children do better with consistency in their lives, and this is a value I always strive for in my own life.

Communication is critical here. As much as possible, "pregame" with each other about your desires and goals for your children. You probably have a general idea of how you feel about certain aspects of parenting, but discussing it clearly and honestly ahead of time will make it easier when difficult parenting situations arise—and they *will* arise, often in ways you never imagined. When you find your heart racing and you and your spouse are giving each other a look that says, "Oh no, what do we do next?" you'll be able to talk it through and solve the problem together.

For example, let's say your 12-year-old daughter approaches you and announces she wants to wear makeup. I encourage parents to take a step back and remove themselves from the situation so they can talk with each other and process their thoughts on the topic. Then agree to a plan of action. This doesn't have to be an immediate answer.

A perfectly good plan could be "Mommy and Daddy want to think this over for a few days and then get back to you."

Inevitably there will be situations that you and your spouse don't agree on or feel you don't have enough time to address properly. In those situations, it's imperative not to argue in front of your children. Attempt to pull from other conversations you've had that may recall your values on certain topics. Also be content with giving a temporary answer and communicating that to your child so they know what to expect. When you have the time, process and sort through the topic with your spouse and come up with a more definitive answer. As long as the two of you are intentional about being on the same page, you will win in parenting.

What does this look like in practice? Let's say a husband and wife have to make a quick decision about who their child's teacher will be next school year.

HUSBAND: *Our daughter is really good at math, but she struggles more with reading.*

WIFE: *Very true. That's why I'm thinking a teacher with high reading scores would be best, because she's already strong in math.*

HUSBAND: *That makes sense. It looks like Mr. Green has the highest reading scores, but I've heard that he's not as structured and doesn't run as tight of a ship.*

WIFE: *And at the last parent-teacher conference, they told us our daughter performs best in highly structured environments. What do you think about going with Mrs. Mochizuki, since she has the second highest reading scores and a very structured classroom?*

HUSBAND: *I think that's a smart move! Great teamwork, honey.*

As you see, this was an off-the-cuff conversation about parenting that had to be resolved quickly. Both parents used assertiveness with compassion, active listening skills, and knowledge from previous conversations in order to make a decision in the moment.

It Takes a Village

There's an old proverb that says it takes a village to raise a child. It means that in order for a child to grow up and learn everything they need to know in a safe and healthy environment, they need to interact with their whole community, not just their parents. I truly believe in and practice this proverb. Raising three children, we depend heavily on our parents, siblings, and close friends—and the children are better for it. Attempting to parent in isolation can cause undue stress, anxiety, and frustration. We all need each other, and that doesn't stop at rearing children.

As a couple, identify who your "village" is. If possible, this should include people from both sides of the child's family. You should both agree that everyone you list is safe for your children to be around. They should be people you both trust who have your children's best interests at heart and would never harm your children.

RECOMMITTING

It's possible that while you've been fighting for your marriage and overcoming challenges within it, other aspects of life have fallen by the wayside. So maybe you've made the choice to recommit to teamwork by agreeing to work on your marriage and reignite the love and fire despite the challenges you've faced.

Right or wrong, some of your family members may not have forgiven your spouse if they committed serious transgressions but have now repented and made amends. If you made your family aware of these challenges, it's important that you also make them aware of your recommitment to teamwork. It is your responsibility to inform them of the recommitment and ask them to support you. If they choose not to, then it may be necessary to love them from afar until they can agree to that recommitment, because your fight for your marriage must take precedence. Teammates have to work together whether the crowd is cheering or booing. (Note that this does *not* apply in cases where a spouse is abusive. See page 128 for more information.)

BE A BETTER LISTENER

In marriage, we have to commit to always becoming a better version of ourselves so that our marriages grow stronger and stronger. That's how we glorify God with our marriages. As we discussed in chapter 2, communication is the foundation of every marriage. Recall that there are two very basic communication strategies that we must use to better hear and understand each other. Being an active listener is critical to any relationship. In your effort to be a better spouse, make a commitment to be a better listener.

If both of you make this commitment, then you'll be confident that at a minimum, your heart and emotions will be heard. It can be hard to put your foot in first because you may be afraid that your spouse won't put their foot in as well. But this is the type of teamwork necessary for strong marriages. Often, when people are recovering from past hurts, they're afraid to engage in teamwork. But if both spouses trust that the other is committed to teamwork, then they'll be better able to leap in themselves.

COMMITTED ACTION

We've learned a lot about teamwork in this chapter. Here are a few things you can take away and apply to your marriage right now to begin to change your family dynamics.

1. Remember that you are a team! Even when you're arguing and can't seem to agree on things, your mission is still the same. Gently remind your spouse when they're not acting as a teammate. Your enemy is outside your house, not inside your bedroom.

2. Serve each other as Jesus serves us! Give with a cheerful heart and be a "helpmeet" through your actions, not just your words.

3. Don't be rigid in your roles. Know your role and play it to the best of your ability, but also be flexible and open to adjusting or swapping roles as the needs in your family change.

*I will exalt you, Lord . . . I called
to you for help, and you healed me.*

Psalm 30:1-2

CHAPTER SIX

DEALING WITH DIFFICULT CONDITIONS

SO FAR WE'VE FOCUSED ON HOW TO overcome the most common marital issues like a lack of communication or unhealthy fighting habits. But what if you have even bigger problems to deal with, like infidelity, addiction, or mental illness? This chapter will tackle those difficult conditions and what to do about them.

THE BIG STUFF

This next chapter is about difficult material, and it will likely be challenging to read, digest, and apply. It may trigger strong emotions for you about experiences you're currently having or have had in the past. If you find yourself becoming angry, reflect back on chapter 3 and the strategies you learned on how to fight fair, including taking a time-out (see page 61). For other emotions such as sadness and anxiety, consider deep breathing, journaling your emotions, and, of course, praying to God and casting your cares on Him. Remember, these are short-term strategies to help you deal with overwhelming emotions in the moment. The problems we'll be discussing will require much more time and effort to deal with in the long run.

Here's a preview of the issues we'll be looking at.

- **Infidelity** is also known as cheating, adultery, or unfaithfulness. Sometimes infidelity is straightforward, like when a person has sex with someone other than their spouse. Other times it's in a gray area, like when a spouse is sending inappropriate text messages to someone outside the marriage. For many, infidelity is one of the worst forms of betrayal of trust. The pain that comes with it typically requires some degree of counseling for both parties to get on the other side of the hurt.
- **Addiction** is defined by the American Psychiatric Association as "a brain disease that is manifested by compulsive substance use despite harmful consequence." The most common form of addiction is the abuse of substances like drugs and alcohol, but people

can also be addicted to certain behaviors like gambling, shopping, and sex. There are therapeutic programs for almost every type of addiction that exists. Some are outpatient and some are inpatient, and although you may not find the one that fits you best on your first try, remember that any decision to get help is a good choice.

- **Mental illness** can encompass a wide range of conditions that affect mood, thinking, and behavior. Those disorders can vary from depression and anxiety to bipolar disorder or various other mood disorders, and they are defined by their ability to cause significant distress and impair functioning. There are a variety of treatments for mental health issues, including psychotherapy, medication, and talk therapy, to name a few of the most popular.
- **Abuse** comes in many forms. When we hear the word "abuse," we tend to think of physical abuse, but emotional, verbal, financial, and sexual abuse are just as real and serious. Abuse is typically about power and control. Any couple who is experiencing abuse should see a therapist for a diagnostic assessment to help them determine the best course of action. In most cases of abuse, the right course of action is separation.

Note that there are many reasons a marriage can fall apart, and it's usually not because of a single problem. If infidelity is an issue in your marriage, for example, it's not happening in a vacuum; there are probably many layers to the problem, including issues with communication and trust. Couples counseling and/or individual therapy can address all the layers, big and small, and for the kinds of things we're talking about in this chapter, one or both is almost always necessary.

THE UNFAITHFUL SPOUSE

Infidelity is the number one reason that I see couples for marital counseling. The American Association for Marriage and Family Therapy reports that "15 percent of women and 25 percent of men have experienced intercourse outside of their long-term relationship. And, by including emotional and sexual intimacies without intercourse, these percentages increase by 20 percent."

Infidelity is one of the most egregious acts we can commit against our spouse, because it violates their trust to the core. As writer Lesli White points out, it's such a serious violation that it's "one of the most frequently and severely condemned sins in the Bible. Adultery is mentioned 52 times, including in the 10 Commandments, all four Gospels, and 10 other books of the Bible."

But the good news is that recovery and reconciliation are very possible, even after infidelity. There is work to be done by both parties to save the marriage, but it can be done—and often is. From a professional perspective, I can tell you that with faith in God and lots of hard, therapeutic work, your marriage can get through anything, including infidelity.

Stopping Infidelity Before It Starts

It's important to understand that infidelity comes in different forms. There are physical affairs and emotional affairs and everything in between. Emotional affairs often lead to physical affairs if they're allowed to develop, which is why we should work to set up healthy emotional boundaries with people outside of our marriages. I don't want to insinuate that people can't be human. It's normal to have thoughts about other people, to find others attractive, to meet people you like and want to get to know better. But what's important is not to act in a way that could jeopardize your marriage.

All couples have their own rules about how to handle relationships with people outside the marriage, and couples need to communicate clearly about it so that their expectations are aligned. For example, when it comes to friends of the opposite sex, what activities are appropriate? Some couples may not be comfortable if their partner spends time alone with a person of the opposite sex. Some have different rules regarding friends from earlier in life versus friends made after the marriage began. Different sets of rules work better for different couples, but the important thing is that you discuss this and that you both have clarity on whatever you decide.

It may seem silly to take the time to engage in conversations about something as small as having lunch with a friend, but I assure you, you'd rather feel a little silly now than have a serious heartache down the line. Minor misunderstandings can grow into major challenges if they aren't addressed. This is true in any area of a couple's relationship, but especially this one. Instead of assuming your partner is comfortable or uncomfortable with the same things you are, have an open and honest conversation about it.

When having this conversation, be careful not to assume that every emotion you have requires your spouse to change their behavior. If you feel uncomfortable with something your spouse is doing, it may be your own insecurities or hang-ups talking. We want to be careful not to allow our insecurities to lead us into controlling or even abusive behavior. So talk through it, using the communication tools you learned in chapter 2. Inform your spouse of how you feel about a certain situation and why. Your spouse might change their behavior, or it might be an opportunity for them to reassure you. Either way, you won't be able to move forward if you're not having an honest conversation based on trust.

Broken Trust

Infidelity breaks all levels of trust. It usually involves lies, sneaking around, and making up cover stories, so on top of the devastating betrayal of the infidelity itself, it can also destroy your trust in everything your spouse does and says.

As an example, let's look at Ken and Stephanie. Stephanie cheated on Ken with a colleague, and Ken is struggling to forgive her. He has threatened her with divorce at least twice a week for the last several months. He doesn't want his marriage to end, but he's struggling to believe that Stephanie will begin to be truthful. Stephanie told him that her affair with her colleague was a onetime thing, but Ken later found emails between her and the colleague that spanned over six months and indicated that they were together more than one night. Ken is now struggling to trust Stephanie in many different areas of their relationship—intimacy, her work schedule, finances, and more. If she was dishonest even when "coming clean," what else is she being dishonest about?

To begin to rebuild trust, a couple needs to be open, honest, and vulnerable with each other. This is often difficult for both parties, due to shame and hurt, but it's not at all impossible. People *can* change their behavior, especially with professional help. I have counseled *many* couples through infidelity and have seen them come out on the other side emotionally healthy and trusting each other again.

Forgiveness

God calls on us to forgive if we wish to be forgiven (Matthew 6:14). When dealing with infidelity, I encourage you to remember the work that God has done for us. He has forgiven us time and time again, even when we've done things that others might deem unforgivable. He looks beyond our faults to see who He made us to be, not just the sum total of our mistakes. He searches our hearts for the good that we do so He can reward our intent. I urge you to find forgiveness in your heart for your spouse, choose to see them for who God has made them, and remember the reasons you married them in the first place. If you want to keep fighting for your marriage, forgiveness is a necessary step on the road to rebuilding trust after infidelity.

That said, it's important to note that forgiveness and moving forward in a marriage are actually two separate issues. Even if you forgive your spouse for infidelity, you may ultimately still end up choosing to divorce. Some factors that people consider when making this choice include the length of the infidelity, the quantity of affairs, whether an unfaithful spouse continues cheating behaviors, any children created outside of the marriage, and the risk of health issues (such as sexually transmitted infections). In the end, each couple must decide for themselves if they can forgive and move forward with each other, or if they must forgive and move on from each other.

People typically choose divorce for one of two reasons. Either you or your spouse believe there is no hope for the marriage to be repaired, or you or your spouse aren't willing to do the heavy lifting required to repair the marriage. The first is a lack of faith, and the second is a lack of work. The book of James reminds us that our works are an outgrowth of our faith: "Show me your faith without deeds, and I will show you my faith by my deeds" (James 2:18). There is no right or wrong choice. God gives us free will, after all! However, we also know how pleased God's heart is when we can push through, work hard, have faith, and restore our marriages.

THE SPOUSE WITH ADDICTION

Addictions can be one of the most difficult challenges for a married couple. According to one 18-year-long national study, "'drinking and drug use' was the third most commonly cited cause of divorce, following infidelity and incompatibility." Many couples are unable to withstand the stress, despair, anxiety, and unhappiness that addiction can cause.

Addiction is a disease that is so pervasively hurtful, confusing, and overwhelming that even the brightest and most educated people can have difficulty admitting that their spouse is addicted to alcohol or another substance. It causes so much shame for the addicted individual that they often keep their behavior a secret and lie to cover it up until they just can't keep it behind closed doors any longer—like when a serious addiction starts affecting finances, material possessions, or even physical appearance.

Any time you have secrets and lies in a marriage (whether that's because of infidelity, addiction, or something else entirely), you're destined to have some level of turmoil. As the secrets and lies are brought to light, the other partner begins to lose trust and question the relationship, even sometimes accusing the addicted person of other transgressions because they don't know or understand what's really going on.

Treat It Like a Disease

Addiction is a chronic disease not unlike cancer or diabetes. Research has shown that addiction is affected by both genetic and environmental factors. No one actively chooses to be an addict, and conversely, once you've become addicted to a substance, you usually can't just choose to stop. As the National Institute on Drug Abuse puts it, "Many people . . . mistakenly think that those who use drugs lack moral principles or willpower and that they could stop their drug use simply by choosing to. In reality, drug addiction is a complex disease, and quitting usually takes more than good intentions or a strong will. Drugs change the brain in ways that make quitting hard, even for those who want to."

This can be a hard thing to wrap your head around if you're married to someone whose addiction is affecting your life. While it is gravely important that the person with addiction seek professional treatment and help, there is also work that their spouse must do, and a lot of it revolves around understanding substance abuse so you can change your perspective and see it as a disease rather than a choice. If your spouse were to develop cancer, would you help them through treatment by saying things like "Come on, just feel better" or "Grow your hair back out"? I don't believe you would. I think patience and compassion would be at the top of your list—and those are the traits you'll need when married to someone with addiction.

Here are some additional steps to take in addition to shifting your perspective:

- Remind yourself that your spouse is not using on purpose.
- Encourage your spouse to get professional help through substance-abuse treatment.
- Get help for yourself through treatment for family members of substance abusers.
- Remind yourself that treatment is a process, and relapses are likely.
- Be patient with your spouse and yourself.
- If necessary, protect yourself, your children, and your financial and material assets.

Addiction is a very serious disease to battle, but it is possible to overcome. Remember, God tells us that "faith without works is dead" (James 2:26, NKJV). So pray, keep the faith, and do the work together. Now we will explore recommendations for where to start.

Tough Love

A person in the throes of addiction may be doing damage to their marriage, family, and life that they would never do while sober. Your support can be invaluable in helping your spouse recover from their addiction, but *supporting* them doesn't mean *enabling* them. If you overlook or go along with their behavior, even as it wreaks havoc, you're not actually doing a kindness for your spouse. You're just making it easier for them to continue further down the path of addiction. By the same token, protecting yourself and your family does not mean you're unkind or that you don't love your spouse. Sometimes tough love is the kind of love that's required.

Here are some ways you can show tough love, based on recommendations from the prominent addiction treatment center JourneyPure:

- Your spouse will need professional help to end their addiction, but *you* can benefit from professional help, too. Seek help through individual counseling or a community support group like Al-Anon.
- If you have kids, make sure they receive help as well.
- Practice "detaching with love." Remove yourself from situations where you might enable your spouse's addiction. For example, if your spouse is an alcoholic and asks you to buy alcohol, don't.
- Be assertive but compassionate in expressing your emotions about the substance abuse and how it has affected you, your family, and your marriage.
- If you're serious, you can use ultimatums, but they *must* be followed up by action. If you say, "The next time this happens, I'm going to leave," but then don't leave, it only teaches your spouse that their actions don't really have consequences.
- Similarly, don't cover up or make excuses for their behavior with others. Allow them to feel the consequences of using.
- Finally, do not compromise your health or sanity for the sake of your spouse's addiction. Their well-being is important, but so is yours.

Getting Help

If you are the spouse with the addiction, it is time to get help—not just for your marriage but for every part of your life. Professional treatment can help you break the cycle of addiction. Start with detox, and then get into an outpatient or inpatient treatment program, depending on your individual needs.

Your treatment should involve diving deep into the issues underlying your addiction. There are many reasons people abuse substances. What are yours? Once you learn them, you can explore the events or situations that trigger you to turn to substances. Exploring your triggers is one of the most liberating parts of treatment because it lets you develop coping skills for exactly the situations in which you need them. These coping skills will lead you to healthier habits and practices so you can live an overall happier and more productive life.

The Serenity Prayer

The Serenity Prayer is not found in the Bible. Based on the words of the theologian Reinhold Niebuhr, it's commonly used in 12-step programs like Alcoholics Anonymous to help remind addicts to seek guidance from a higher power. It reads:

*God, grant me the serenity to accept the things
I cannot change,
Courage to change the things I can,
And wisdom to know the difference.*

If you're married to an addict, this prayer can be valuable to you, too. Read it aloud and think about what it means for you. What are you attempting to solve for your spouse that only they can solve for themselves? What are you fighting to change about your spouse that you need to take a step back from? We can and should support our spouses, but we can't be their saviors; only God can do that.

THE SPOUSE WITH MENTAL ILLNESS

When one spouse is living with mental health issues, it can put strain on a marriage. The term "mental health issues" encompasses a lot of different things. It could mean depression or anxiety. It could mean bipolar disorder or post-traumatic stress disorder. These issues could be mild or severe. As with addiction, it's important to remember that mental illness is not the consequence of poor choices. You can remain a team through these challenges, remembering that you are each other's helpmeets.

If your spouse is going through long-term or short-term mental health issues, it can be easy to get caught up in wondering how and why. You care about your spouse, so of course you want to understand the source of their pain and help them solve it. This is commendable! But the causes of mental illness are often unknowable, and figuring them out isn't a cure. A better way to help your spouse is to accept what is and work on how to move forward. Let's look at some ways to do this.

Diagnosis and Treatment

It's important for anyone with a mental illness to get a proper diagnosis and proper professional treatment. Because a lot of these issues start with sadness and/or anxiety, it can often seem like your spouse is just "having a few bad days" or "going through a rough patch." If you think your spouse may be experiencing a mental health problem, gently encourage them to seek help. And if you think you're experiencing a mental health problem, let your partner know what's going on, inform them of your symptoms, and allow them to help you through the process of seeking help.

Your relationship with God will be necessary on this journey, but after you get down on your knees and pray, it's time to stand up and put your faith to work. Getting the proper mental health care from a professional is the work. There might be some trial and error during the process, but getting the right diagnosis and treatment plan can be highly effective. God has gifted medical experts with the credentials to be a transport for this healing. We are abundantly blessed to have Jesus and therapy!

Don't Minimize the Problem

One of the most harmful things you can do to someone going through a mental health crisis is to minimize it. Too often, people tell their loved ones things like "Things can't be that bad," "I'm tired of seeing you sad," "Stop complaining," or "Pray harder, you must be living in sin." We may not realize it, but these kinds of statements can be extremely detrimental. Mental illness is as real as any other illness like the flu or cancer. If we don't take it seriously, the consequences can be grave. Not all couples recite traditional vows at their wedding, but most of us would agree we intend to be with our spouse "in sickness and in health," so love your spouse through their sickness. I'm not saying it's up to you to solve your spouse's mental health problems for them—only they can do that, working with a professional. What I am saying is that your support and understanding are crucial. Don't infantilize your spouse or brush off their concerns.

Be a Good Listener

Being a good listener is a necessary part of being a good partner in any marriage, but during mental health challenges, it's even more important. When a spouse is experiencing, say, major depression, they may question your love for and commitment to them or their love for and commitment to you. Instead of becoming offended, try to understand that there are factors outside your control affecting your spouse's thought processes. The situation will require patience as you navigate diagnosis and treatment as a team.

THE ABUSIVE SPOUSE

Abuse is different from the other difficulties we've explored so far. Couples can and often do overcome infidelity, addiction, and mental illness in a marriage, but it's rare for an abuser to change their ways. The strategies that we've covered in such detail for other marital problems—assertiveness with compassion, openness and honesty, patience and understanding—don't work with abuse. If you are experiencing abuse within your marriage, you don't need to seek marital counseling but rather individual domestic violence services and counseling. For that reason, this section will be less about tools to deal with abuse and more about tools to recognize it and understand how it works. Abuse can take many forms, but they all stem from a place of insecurity and represent poor attempts by one spouse to gain power and control over the other.

If you're in immediate danger, please call 911. If it is possible and safe, remove yourself from the situation. Reach out to the National Domestic Violence Hotline at TheHotline.org or 1-800-799-7233 for more help.

Physical Abuse

Physical abuse is an intentional act causing physical injury or trauma, and it's often the first thing we think of when we hear the word "abuse." It includes pushing, hitting, kicking, spitting, pinching, and more. As domestic violence shelter The Women's Safe House (TWSH) puts it, this kind of violence "occurs when one person feels entitled to power and control over their partner and chooses to use abuse to gain and maintain that control." Typically, the abuser, in some misconception, feels powerless and uses violence to regain a sense of power. TWSH adds that "[i]n relationships where domestic violence exists, violence is not equal, even if the victim fights back or instigates violence in an effort to defuse a situation. There is always one person who is the primary, constant source of power, control, and abuse in the relationship."

Emotional and Verbal Abuse

Emotional abuse and verbal abuse are closely related and sometimes overlapping. They use emotions and words as weapons rather than physical harm, but they come from the same attempt to control, and they're just as real as physical abuse. Almost 100 percent of the time, if physical abuse is occurring, emotional abuse is occurring, too.

Forms of emotional and verbal abuse include accusing, blaming, insulting, name-calling, and threatening physical harm. It's not uncommon for us to see someone try to control what their spouse wears, where they can go, and who they interact with. In extreme cases, we see an abusive spouse attempt to isolate their partner by forcing them to "cut off" family and friends. The spouse who is being controlled can sometimes mistake this behavior for a deep love, when in fact it's the opposite. Emotional and verbal abuse can lead to feelings of sadness, unworthiness, and despair. It's often used as a form of coercion to make the victim too afraid to leave.

If your spouse is engaging in emotional and/or verbal abuse, it's important to remember that although you may be the target of their attacks, you are not the problem, no matter how many times your perpetrator may try to convince you that you are. It's also important to remember that you cannot reason with someone amid irrational anger. It's more productive to keep quiet until you can safely remove yourself from the situation and seek safety.

If you are the person who is inflicting verbal abuse on your spouse, you need to seek help immediately through professional counseling.

Financial Abuse

Financial abuse is when one spouse asserts power and control over the other using money, and it's often viewed as the "hidden" form of abuse because it's rarely reported. It often takes the form of one spouse not allowing the other to work so that they lack their own funds and have to depend on the abuser. I've also seen abusers require that all paychecks be turned over to them and that all bank accounts and large loans (like mortgages) be in their name. Other forms of financial abuse include coercing a spouse into signing financial documents, committing bank fraud, or cashing checks without the victim's permission.

Sexual Abuse

Sexual assault occurs when one person coerces or physically forces another person to engage in a sexual act without their consent.

One of the biggest misconceptions about sexual abuse is that it can't occur within a marriage. It can and it does. And the worst part is that sometimes people use the Bible to try to justify it. We have to be careful not to use scriptures such as Hebrews 13:4, which tells us that the marriage bed is "undefiled" (KJV), as a way to say, "Nothing I do to my spouse sexually could be wrong, because we're married." To the contrary, I believe that to abuse or misuse God's gift of sex is to defile the marriage bed. If your sexual desires are going unmet, that means it's an opportunity to communicate with compassion and care using the strategies from chapter 4 (see page 81). It does not mean you have permission to make your spouse meet those needs against their will. If you pressure or force your spouse to participate in sexual activity that they don't want, that's sexual abuse.

Beyond your marriage, if you suspect that your partner is committing any form of sexual abuse toward another person—in your home or otherwise—seek help immediately.

ADDRESSING HEAVY PROBLEMS HEAD-ON

You know from previous chapters that the best way to deal with any issue in a marriage is to address it head-on. The same goes for the issues in this chapter, but it can be intimidating to take on such heavy problems. This section will focus on concepts and tools you can use to slay these dragons.

Don't Be an Enabler

We've touched on this before, but it bears repeating. An enabler is someone who, often without meaning to, encourages another person's negative or self-destructive behavior. If your spouse has an addiction or mental health diagnosis, this is a term you need to get familiar with. It's easy to slip into the enabler role with your spouse because you love them and you want to see them happy. But there are times when what makes someone happy in the short term is actually unhealthy for them. I encourage you to resist the urge to enable, knowing that although your efforts may seem to make your spouse less happy in the moment, you're actually aiding their long-term happiness.

Communicate Clearly

Remember when we discussed communicating with clarity, intentionality, assertiveness, and compassion? That becomes even more true the bigger the problem gets.

Let's say that Tara has been unhappy with Andrew's drinking for years but has never come right out and stated it. One day she gets frustrated and feels like she can't take it anymore.

TARA: *I hate who you've become! You don't care about me. You prioritize all the wrong things and put everything else before me.*

Now let's look at a different way to communicate those feelings.

TARA: *I feel neglected when you drink alcohol. It seems like nothing else matters to you when you're drinking, not even me. I want to feel close to you, the way I used to. Can we talk about the frequency of your drinking?*

What if Tara were clearer in her communication? What if she'd brought it up when she first started feeling it, instead of after years of anger? No, it wouldn't have magically cured Andrew's addiction, but it could have helped steer their marriage toward the right path earlier. Be honest, open, and expressive with your feelings. Your spouse needs your assertive compassion as well as actions that match your words.

Engage the Community

Matthew 18:15–17 says, "If your brother or sister sins, go and point out their fault, just between the two of you. If they listen to you, you have won them over. But if they will not listen, take one or two others along so that 'every matter may be established by the testimony of two or three witnesses.' If they still refuse to listen, tell it to the church." If communication between you and your spouse breaks down, it may be necessary to engage the community. Note that it's important for us to follow God's Word and have one-on-one conversations with our spouse before bringing in people from outside the marriage. You don't want to railroad your spouse with community involvement before you give them a chance to fix things just between the two of you. But when you've genuinely obeyed verse 15 and it hasn't worked, then it may be time to move to verses 16 and 17, making sure that the community members you involve not only love your spouse but also will hold them accountable and not enable any negative behavior.

What does engaging the community look like? Let's return to Tara and Andrew from our last example. Let's say that Tara chose the second option in that example and communicated with assertiveness and compassion early and often. After those conversations, she'd need to allow Andrew some time to get the help he needs and put recovery strategies in place. But if he refused to listen and showed no signs of changing his behavior, then she could begin engaging the community. She might speak to the pastor at their church, an elder she trusts, or even a marriage ministry leader. She might also go to family members who love and support

Andrew. These are all people who might have experience finding solutions to these kinds of issues or who can try communicating directly with Andrew themselves. Of course, the community might not be able to get through to your spouse, either, but it is one tool in your toolbox.

PRACTICE SELF-CARE

Luke 5:16 says that "Jesus often withdrew to lonely places and prayed." In this verse, the word "lonely" refers to solitude. Jesus went to places where he could be alone, rest, and communicate with His Father. When you're in the midst of thorny issues like the ones covered in this chapter, it's important for you to have restorative practices like Jesus did.

As a matter of fact, God wants you to do so! Let's remember Mark 6:31, when the disciples had just returned from traveling from village to village, preaching and performing miracles. "Then, because so many people were coming and going that they did not even have a chance to eat, he said to them, 'Come with me by yourselves to a quiet place and get some rest.'" As a busy spouse, parent, and career woman, I love that God calls for me to rest!

Some people mistakenly believe that the term "self-care" refers to indulging in anything you want for self-gratification. But going out and buying fancy clothing or lavish gifts does not constitute self-care. On the contrary, self-care means affirming yourself through positive self-talk, healthy boundaries, and rest that comforts your spirit. It allows God to affirm you through His word.

The first step in practicing self-care is acknowledging that you need it. Imagine a teacup sitting on a saucer. Now imagine pouring tea into the cup until it overflows and spills onto the saucer. The tea in the cup belongs to you and you only. The tea on the saucer is what you have available to share with others, like your spouse. What I see most often in private practice is one spouse trying to pour out tea for the other spouse, even though their own teacup is nearly empty. They're trying to be generous, which is admirable, but they have nothing to give, and pretty soon there's no tea for anyone.

Retreating to a "lonely place" like Jesus and his disciples did lets you replenish your cup with God's love, care, and strength. When we fill our own cups, we have enough to overflow with help for others and fulfill His mission of being helpmeets for each other.

Work on Yourself

Matthew 7:3 reminds us to look at the plank in our own eye before looking at the speck of sawdust in someone else's. We all have challenges in our lives. No one is exempt from difficulties. Yours may not be infidelity, addiction, or mental illness, but it is something. If your spouse is exhibiting these destructive behaviors, working on yourself might mean improving the way you respond and engaging in healthy communication and boundary-setting rather than enabling or lashing out.

Note that this idea does not apply when dealing with an abusive spouse. Abuse is unrelated to the victim's actions and is solely about power, control, and the abuser's inability to manage their own emotions. We all need to work on our character flaws, but no character flaw gives your spouse the right to abuse you.

FIRST STEPS

This chapter was loaded with some very heavy material. Allow yourself to be introspective for a moment and think about what you've read. Are you living in any of these situations? Have you or your spouse been struggling with infidelity, addiction, or mental health issues? What about abuse?

If so, it's time to take action. Grab your journal or notebook, because we're going to start creating a plan. Write down at least three steps or things you need to do to help yourself and your marriage. These can be simple and relatively small, like "Research couples counselors in my area," followed by "Set an appointment with a couples counselor." Pray over your plan and ask God to give you further guidance with it. Each day, look at your plan and begin to put the steps into action. As you take more steps, you'll gain more strength and knowledge, which will allow you to take even more steps as you keep moving forward into a better marriage.

COMMITTED ACTION

This may have been a difficult chapter. If you're dealing with any of the serious issues we covered in your marriage, you're probably still digesting what you read. A question I often hear from individuals facing tough issues who are committed to trying to heal their relationship is "How long should I wait?" They want to save their marriage and they're doing their part, but they're awaiting the same commitment to change from their partner. The answer to that question is within yourself. From a Christian perspective, there are certain things that justify divorce. But if you are not being physically, sexually, or psychologically harmed, I encourage all couples to push through together until change comes. To that end, these are a few of the strategies you can start applying to your marriage right away.

1. Open up clear lines of communication with your spouse. Be clear, upfront, and compassionate about infidelity and other serious issues.

2. Develop a self-care plan. Remember, self-care doesn't mean buying yourself new things. It means caring for your emotional health. Go to your "lonely place" and communicate with God. Identify what you need and allow Him to "fill your teacup."

3. Seek professional help in the form of individual and/or couples counseling. Therapy can be helpful for many issues, but especially the ones we talked about in this chapter.

4. Last but certainly not least, if you are in an abusive relationship, seek help as soon as possible from a therapist who specializes in domestic violence. If you're not sure where to find one, start by contacting the National Domestic Violence Hotline at TheHotline.org or 1-800-799-7233. Remember, abuse is never okay and never your fault. Your safety comes first.

But I trust in your unfailing love;
my heart rejoices in your salvation.

Psalm 13:5

CHAPTER SEVEN

REBUILDING TRUST

OVER THE COURSE OF THIS BOOK WE'VE learned how to communicate better, fight fair, and tackle problems big and small. But once you've started addressing those problems, how do you move forward? This chapter will focus on how to reestablish trust in your relationship, especially after a major betrayal, so that you and your partner can begin healing from the past and building your future together.

TRUST IS EVERYTHING

Trust is fundamental to any relationship. To have true emotional intimacy with your spouse, you have to be secure in the knowledge that your partner has your best interests at heart and won't intentionally try to hurt you. If one of you accidentally hurts the other, you have to be able to trust that they'll genuinely apologize and work hard to keep it from happening again. Trust also lets you both lead connected but independent lives, instead of constantly worrying that your spouse is secretly cheating, racking up debt, and so on.

Without trust, you can't have *agape* love—the purest form of unconditional love, the kind God has for us. The Bible shows us what trust looks like within a relationship based on His *agape* love toward us: "Trust in the Lord with all your heart and lean not on your own understanding" (Proverbs 3:5).

When the trust between a husband and wife has been broken, especially by egregious acts like some of those covered in chapter 6, it's hard to repair. But that doesn't mean it's impossible, and with work, both spouses can commit themselves to the process of rebuilding trust. Let's dive deeper into what that means.

Acknowledge and Release the Hurt

Acknowledging the hurt—whether it's based on feelings of anger, abandonment, anxiety, or anything else—is the first step in the healing process. When your spouse ignores your feelings no matter what you do, it's painful and often infuriating. If you and your partner can't trust each other with the basic reality of acknowledging each other's feelings, then it's going to be impossible to address those feelings and move forward. But when they really see what you're going through and genuinely want to make it better, it's easier to release that hurt and start to rebuild.

Becky, for example, has been damaged by her husband John's marijuana addiction. Initially John struggled to understand why the situation was so painful for her. After all, it was *his* addiction. He figured he was only hurting *himself* with the drug, not her. In order to move forward as a couple, they needed to address the hurt Becky felt, but they couldn't do that if John wouldn't even believe that she was hurt.

When they made it into couples therapy, their counselor helped John come to terms with the fact that his addiction affects everyone who's close to him, especially his wife.

BECKY: *Baby, I've been so upset at you! I felt you chose drugs over me, and it hurt. I've walked around for months angry at you for not choosing me.*

JOHN: *I never knew you felt I chose drugs over you. I would never intentionally do that. It wasn't a matter of putting you first. I always want to put you first. But the addiction was so strong that I often felt out of control. I didn't realize how it was making you feel. I'm sorry.*

Once all the emotions were out in the open, they both felt better and were able to begin the process of letting the hurt feelings go. When John was able to fully digest Becky's hurt, it allowed him to address the damage his addiction had done not just to himself but also to his marriage.

That doesn't mean that one single conversation solves all the problems, or that hurt and anger won't come up again during the healing process. But if you're making the choice to stay with your spouse, then acknowledging and releasing the hurt of whatever has come between you is a necessary step.

Make Changes

Once you've started to acknowledge and release the hurt, it's time to make changes in your behavior. As I've mentioned, James 2:26 tells us that faith without works is dead; works are the means by which we express our faith. So often, we think it's enough to feel faithful. We say things like "God, I trust You to see us through these challenges" or "God, I trust You to make a way out of no way." That faith is necessary, but why do we think God gave us free will? It's because He doesn't force us to do anything. He wants us to choose to do the right thing and apply our faith to our lives with our actions. Even if you genuinely apologize to your spouse for the ways you've wronged them, you also have to make changes so that you stop wronging them.

This goes for both spouses. Even if only one spouse has committed a grave error like being unfaithful, both spouses need to change how they act so that the relationship becomes healthier from both sides.

If we take our example couple John and Becky, John had to rebuild trust with Becky by following through on his words with his actions. He had to quit using marijuana and stop the lying and sneaking around that his addiction required. He had to become a man of his word, even just on simple things like coming home from work on time or actually going to social events he'd agreed to attend. Becky also had to make changes and put in the work to rebuild trust with John. For her, that meant that once he'd demonstrated he was following through, she stopped constantly calling him to check in on his whereabouts and accusing him of lies. As you can imagine, if either one of them stopped doing their share of the work, it would throw the entire cycle off. If Becky kept accusing John of things he wasn't doing, he wouldn't be able to trust her. If John went back to using drugs and lying, Becky wouldn't be able to trust him. They both need to change their behavior in order to rebuild trust.

EARN IT BACK

Many people believe that once trust is broken, it's gone forever. But trust absolutely can be rebuilt. If you've broken your spouse's trust, the strategies you'll need to earn it back aren't complicated, but they do require some heavy lifting. Here are a few of them.

1. Communication, communication, communication. You can't rebuild trust if you don't communicate what that requires! If one spouse has given the other good reason not to trust them, they should initiate this communication by asking what their spouse feels they can do to earn trust back.

2. Make an effort to do the things your spouse requested. This might mean going to couples therapy together, being open and honest about who you're spending time with, and so on.

3. Keep your word about the little things, too! If you say you'll be home at 7:00 p.m., make an intentional effort to honor that. If you promise to cook dinner, follow through on the promise. If you show consistent behavior with the small things, your spouse can learn to trust you with the big things once again.

Don't Keep Secrets

We often keep secrets because we fear what the repercussions would be if the truth came out. There should be no big secrets between spouses (unless we're talking about something like a surprise party or a nice gift). Moving forward, the couple should commit to laying everything out on the table and being forthright with information. Open lines of communication are a necessity.

This applies even to small secrets. In fact, the things you think are no big deal are often the most important things to share when rebuilding trust. For example, let's say your spouse is expecting you to come home right after work, but you see there's a sale at the shoe store on your commute so you stop to pick up a pair. Buying yourself a new pair of shoes, assuming you can afford them, is not a big deal. But if you're, say, trying to rebuild trust after infidelity, and now you're late coming home and your spouse doesn't know where you are, it's going to be scary and painful for them. How do they know you're not cheating again? A harmless pair of shoes will start to erode any trust you've rebuilt. That's why it's important to commit to not keeping any secrets, even small, innocent ones.

GET NAKED

No, I don't mean that literally. This is an exercise I use with couples in my private practice, and I call it "Get Naked" because it requires you to be vulnerable and trust your spouse with your heart as you express your innermost thoughts, feelings, and emotions—as if you were getting emotionally naked. Here's how to do it.

On notecards or scraps of paper, write the following words:

- Accessible
- Ready
- Open
- Sensitive
- Clear
- Responsible
- Receptive
- Willing

Mix the cards up and take turns randomly choosing a card. For each card, describe how you can show *more* of that quality—how you can be *more* sensitive, clear, open, etc. When you've gone through all the cards, discuss how good you were at getting naked!

THE REALITY OF MARRIAGE

Perhaps the biggest misconception that the media gives us about marriage is the concept of "happily ever after" immediately following the "I dos." When I work with couples for premarital counseling, one of the premises we go over is the work of marriage. I always tell them that the work doesn't end the moment you say "I do"—that's when it actually *begins*. Simply getting married is not the prerequisite for happiness.

Now, let's dissect this a little. There's nothing wrong with "happy." It's the "ever after" part that's the problem. You will certainly experience happiness in your marriage. But you will also experience sadness, excitement, frustration, anxiety, surprise, anger, and every other emotion you can think of. There is no one emotion that you'll experience *forever*. So be less concerned about staying happy all the time (which is impossible) and more concerned about being able to manage all the different emotions that life will bring you.

It's easy to think the "honeymoon phase" will last forever. After all, you're madly in love with your best friend! What could be better? But as life happens, it changes our emotions and behaviors. Our spouses won't always behave the way we think they should. Sometimes they'll do the exact opposite! And sometimes they may act downright ugly and hurtful. It's during those times that we must push through, not judge our spouse based on their worst day, and treat them with grace and mercy. The reality of marriage is that it's easy and hard all at the same time. But even when our emotions are changeable, our commitment level has to be consistent so we can work through the darker periods of marriage and get back to the brighter realities.

Self-Work

Another big misconception about marriage is the belief that if your spouse would just change their ways, the relationship would instantly be so much better. As adults, we know that change only happens when an individual wants to change. We can't force change upon others because we don't control them. The only person you can change is yourself. As Matthew 7:5 says, take the plank out of your eye before you look at the speck in someone else's.

What exactly is self-work? Self-work is any action you take toward improving yourself. Maybe for you it's working on patience, learning to handle your emotions, or even developing better financial management skills. The effort that goes into improving yourself, like taking classes or going to therapy, might sometimes feel selfish. But when you improve yourself, you also benefit your spouse and your marriage. That's why it's important to always be working on ourselves. Your spouse's life is directly and indirectly affected by your personal improvement, and vice versa.

Now, I'm not saying that you shouldn't make requests for your spouse to improve in certain areas. You absolutely should, using the assertive but compassionate communication strategies we've discussed. But trying to force it will only bring you greater frustration. Instead, express your desires, and then wait on them to manifest. The cool thing is that there's work you can do during the wait. You can pray for your spouse, assist with love and encouragement, and most importantly, lead by example through your own self-work.

The Soul Mate Myth

Many people are attached to the idea of the "soul mate": that one person somewhere out there who's destined to be their perfect match. Sometimes this idea can give us unrealistic expectations, because we believe that our spouse must have all the correct characteristics and criteria for marriage. Be careful with this perspective, and remember that neither you nor your spouse is perfect—no one is. The reality is that once you enter into marriage, you make the decision to accept your partner, flaws and all.

Release the idea of perfection and adopt the idea of progression. Expecting perfection will almost always leave us disappointed, while working on progression acknowledges that you and your spouse are evolving each day. Instead of leaning on the idea that a harmonious marriage will occur naturally and effortlessly when you're married to your soul mate, lean on the philosophy that you and your spouse are allowed to grow and change in your own right to achieve both personal goals and relationship goals. Trust the places in your marriage where you have strong connections, and continue to work on the places where you struggle.

The Honesty Pact

There is no better answer than an honest one . . . but what I see most often in my practice is that couples will be dishonest for a good reason. Sounds like an oxymoron, right? But I see couples who don't tell the truth for fear that they will hurt, lose, or be judged by their spouse. Those reasons are all completely understandable, but let me tell you: Although being honest may cause discord initially, it's much better to deal with that discord now than to deal with it later when it comes out *and* your spouse knows you've lied about it. Telling the truth the first time around gets you better results in the end.

I've encouraged many couples to make an honesty pact. Make the decision that no matter the topic or situation, you will always be honest with each other. Now, of course, there's some work that goes into the honesty pact, and that's why you must create the space for your spouse to be vulnerable enough to give you the truth. If you're asking your spouse for honesty, make an intentional effort not to fly off the handle if they tell you something uncomfortable. Try to hear them out before you respond. I know that's easier said than done, but making a genuine effort to do this shows love and commitment, even if you don't always succeed. So, yes, I'm asking both you and your spouse to do the work of keeping honesty in your relationship. It will most certainly pay off.

GIVE IT TIME

Rebuilding trust takes time. There's no shortcut you can take or button you can press. It's a process. As we've discussed, everyone deserves grace and mercy. Even if one spouse has forgiven the other for a serious transgression, that doesn't mean everything immediately goes back to normal. When we sin and fall short of God's glory, we can rely on His patience with us. Work on giving your spouse the same patience that you desire from God—and they'll do the same for you.

If You're the Offender

Of course, most marital issues aren't completely one-sided. But if you've committed a serious offense, like infidelity, there are some things you can do to make amends and move forward with your spouse. There are the things we've discussed already, like honesty, realistic expectations, self-work, and releasing hurt. You can also honor reasonable requests your spouse makes (e.g., being transparent about where you are and who you're with, removing passwords on devices, etc.) in order to rebuild trust.

Resist the urge to say things like:

- I've already apologized. Why are we stuck here?
- Just get over it already.
- You're asking for too much!
- I'm not going to check in with you like a child.

Instead, use phrases like:

- Whatever it takes to rebuild your trust in me, I will do it.
- I will never leave the ring. I'm here for the fight.
- This is tough for me, but I understand the purpose.

- Sometimes it's uncomfortable for me to communicate about everything, but it's worth it to feel a little uncomfortable if I get to have you.

This vocabulary will help repair your relationship. It gives your spouse the time and space to heal properly so that trust can be rebuilt, rather than constructing a façade that lets you pretend like everything is fine now even though real trust doesn't exist yet.

If Your Spouse Is the Offender

In the field of social work, we believe that everyone is a product of their environment. Our behaviors are learned, meaning we act based on what we know to be true from our environment. The beauty is that if we can learn a behavior, we can also unlearn it. But you don't learn a habit overnight, and unlearning one takes a long time, too. Have patience with your spouse as they try to improve on bad habits and unhealthy behaviors.

Recall John and Becky, our example couple from earlier working through substance abuse. It would be unrealistic to think that a drug habit will be broken in a week. (In fact, addiction takes much longer to break than most habits.) If John is genuinely trying his best and is showing progress but Becky is still impatient with him, it could become a deal breaker for John.

Let us also recall Romans 12:19, one of many Bible verses that warn against retaliation: "Beloved, never avenge yourselves, but leave it to the wrath of God, for it is written, 'Vengeance is mine, I will repay, says the Lord'" (ESV). God encourages us not to attempt to right a wrong with a wrong. Instead, He implores us to put our trust in Him and allow

Him to take care of the situation. Although retaliation might give you some small gratification in the moment, you will inevitably feel God nudging at your spirit to inform you of your wrongdoing, and your marriage won't get any better.

Swallow Your Pride

Whichever side of the offense you're on, working to rebuild trust requires you to swallow your pride. This can be especially difficult for the spouse who was the offender. They may have to humble themselves when they're asked to change their behavior. Proverbs 16:18 tells us that pride goes before a fall. Oftentimes, pride is the reason we end up in the situation of needing to rebuild trust in the first place. That's how we know it has to die in order to rebuild. In its place, build humility and vulnerability. You'll be going the extra mile, communicating a lot more, being very transparent, and giving more of yourself so that you can show your spouse you want to earn their trust.

THE NEW NORMAL

As a couple works to rebuild trust, a sad reality is that the relationship may never be the same, especially if the offense was egregious. Spend some time discussing how it will be necessary to adjust to a new normal. The hardest pill to swallow for most couples is that the person you are post-offense is likely different from who you were pre-offense. Pain changes who we are. Even after we heal from the pain, we never forget what it felt like, and we never forget the lessons learned from that pain. But that doesn't mean your relationship is over. It just means your relationship will change. Change how? Your communication may change, your intimacy may change, the roles in the relationship may change. It's important to designate a time to have an open and honest conversation about these very issues. When you accept the new normal, you can work on strategies to deal with it.

For example, if one partner was hiding a spending problem that affected the family's finances, the new normal is going to be open financial communication. One strategy to achieve that could be scheduling a weekly money meeting in which you're both completely transparent about the money you brought in and spent that week.

Now, this is not to say that the new normal will be a step down and that you have to get used to a worse life. As a matter of fact, if you follow the techniques in this book, the new normal should be *better* than what you previously had. So even if it feels uncomfortable or exhausting right now, keep pushing. It will pay off in the long run. Your marriage is worth the pivot!

COMMITTED ACTION

This was another heavy chapter, but if you've made it this far in this book, then I imagine it's important to you to fight for your marriage. Right now you might be deep in thought, scared, nervous, or maybe even hopeful. Regardless of your emotions, it's important to know that now is the time to work on your marriage. Even though you may still be digesting some things, there are a few takeaways you can put into action right now as you work to rebuild trust.

1. Identify how you feel and own it. Feel your emotions and acknowledge them. You can't heal from something you can't admit. This goes for both spouses, the offender and the offended. Both people's emotions deserve acknowledgment.

2. Rebuilding trust in your relationship is hard work, but worth it. As you each do your share, remember to be patient and kind with each other. Sit and listen to how your spouse feels, even when you don't like it or agree with it.

3. Be diligently honest and transparent, even about the small stuff that may not have seemed like a big deal before but is now a crucial part of repairing trust.

COMMITTING IN CHRIST

Congratulations! You've reached the end of this book, but the beginning of a new relationship. "What do we do now?" you may be asking. It is my hope that you took great notes and highlighted or underlined the parts of this book that you needed most, and that you will start acting on them.

I'm not oblivious to the difference between reading something and actually applying it to your life, so I will tell you in advance that putting these strategies into practice won't be easy. But it won't be impossible, either. Take your time with yourself as you begin to apply what you've read and learned. Just like anything you're new at, it will take time to master many of these concepts, so be kind and patient with yourself and your spouse.

"Healing" can sometimes be such an overused word that we begin to think of it as a cliché. But if your marriage has experienced challenges, big or small, there is probably some healing to be done. Don't be afraid to seek professional help. Therapy, individually or as a couple, can be a great resource.

Remember that it is not your responsibility to change your spouse—in fact, it's not even possible. Change comes when an individual is ready for it. You can make suggestions for areas of growth and even model the behavior you wish to see, but ultimately the work is theirs to do.

Marriage is a gift from God. It is a beautiful expression of God's love, patience, grace, and sacrifice. Our gift back to Him is the quality of our marriages: the work we put in and the love we share. One thing I've learned is that marriage is not merely for the two people inside it. My private practice, It Takes 2 Marriage Coaching, operates under the premise that if we can improve your marriage, we can improve the lives of your children. Then your children can go out and positively influence the community, and your community can influence the world. Luke 15:10 tells us that the angels rejoice when just one sinner repents from bad things, so we know that when couples begin to live better, godlier marriages, then heaven is in full celebration.

Remember that if you find yourself in a marriage where you are being physically or emotionally harmed, your primary goal should be not to save your marriage but to save yourself. No one deserves to be abused or to feel unsafe, and no one should have to accept a lifetime of unhappiness if, for example, dealing with repeated infidelity. God loves us more than anything and does not want to see His people being hurt or abused.

Considering how important marriage is, I encourage all couples to push through the normal challenges that are bound to occur when two people choose to do life together. I am a firm believer that a couple can overcome nearly any situation they come up against. The quality of your marriage is not based on how many problems you have or how big those problems are, but how you respond to those problems. Be willing to try everything before you try divorce.

There are many times in our lives when we have to pivot: starting a new career, losing a job, the death of a loved one, the birth of a baby. Challenges in marriage are also pivot points. Don't be afraid to do the work, change, and grow. You can alter the trajectory of your marriage and live a reconciled life.

RESOURCES

Celebrate Our Love Couple's Journal: 120 Activities to Make Connecting Fun by Patrice Bush

The 5 Love Languages: The Secret to Love That Lasts by Gary Chapman

Marriage 101: Building A Life Together by Faith by Jewell Powell

The Seven Principles for Making Marriage Work by John Gottman and Nan Silver

The Love Dare by Stephen & Alex Kendrick

Marriage Matters by Tony Evans

ItTakes2MarriageCoaching.com

REFERENCES

AAMFT.org. "Infidelity." Accessed May 3, 2020. AAMFT.org /Consumer_Updates/Infidelity.aspx.

Bevilacqua, Luiz, and David Goldman. "Genes and Addictions." *Clinical Pharmacology & Therapeutics* 85, no. 4 (April 2009): 359–361. doi:10.1038/clpt.2009.6.

Chick, Nancy. "Thinking about One's Thinking: Putting Metacognition into Practice." Vanderbilt University Center for Teaching. Accessed May 3, 2020. CFT.Vanderbilt.edu /guides-sub-pages/metacognition.

Cranford, James A. "DSM-IV Alcohol Dependence and Marital Dissolution: Evidence from the National Epidemiologic Survey on Alcohol and Related Conditions." *Journal of Studies on Alcohol and Drugs* 75, no. 3 (May 2014): 520–529. doi:10.15288/jsad.2014.75.520.

Cutrer, Corrie. "The New Face of Infidelity." *Christianity Today.* May 24, 2016. ChristianityToday.com/women/2015 /november/new-face-of-adultery.html.

DaveRamsey.com. "Money, Marriage, and Communication: What New Research Reveals." February 7, 2018. DaveRamsey .com/research/money-marriage-communication.

DrugAbuse.gov. "Understanding Drug Use and Addiction." National Institute on Drug Abuse. Last modified June 2018. DrugAbuse.gov/publications/drugfacts/understanding -drug-use-addiction.

EmeraldCoastJourneyPure.com. "Do's and Don'ts for Helping Your Addicted Spouse." *JourneyPure.* Accessed May 3, 2020. EmeraldCoastJourneyPure.com /dos-and-donts-for-helping-your-addicted-spouse.

Evans, Jimmy. "Five Rules for Serving Your Spouse." *MarriageToday*. December 20, 2018. MarriageToday.com /marriagehelp/five-rules-serving-spouse.

Forleo, Marie. "Self-Made Millionaire: The Simple Strategy That Helped Increase My Odds of Success by 42%." CNBC. Last modified September 13, 2019. CNBC.com /2019/09/13/self-made-millionaire-how-to-increase -your-odds-of-success-by-42-percent-marie-forleo.html.

Gottman, John. *The Science of Trust*. New York: W.W. Norton, 2011.

Lisitsa, Ellie. "Making Life Dreams Come True: Dreams Within Conflict." The Gottman Institute. January 22, 2013. Gottman.com/blog/make-life-dreams-come-true -dreams-within-conflict.

Masters, William H., and Virginia Johnson. *Human Sexual Response*. Boston: Little, Brown, 1966.

Prepare-Enrich.com. "Workbook for Couples." Accessed May 3, 2020. Prepare-Enrich.com/prepare_enrich_content /reference/parenting_workbook_pe.pdf.

Psychiatry.org. "What Is Addiction?" American Psychiatric Association. Accessed May 3, 2020. Psychiatry.org/patients -families/addiction/what-is-addiction.

Rosenberg, Marshall B. "The 4-Part Nonviolent Communi- cation (NVC) Process." PuddleDancer Press. Accessed May 3, 2020. NonviolentCommunication.com/aboutnvc /4partprocess.htm.

Spangle, Michael L., and Myra W. Isenhart. *Negotiation: Communication for Diverse Settings*. Thousand Oaks, CA: SAGE Publications, 2002.

Spector, Nicole. "Smiling can trick your brain into happiness—and boost your health." NBC. Last modified January 9, 2018. NBCNews.com/better/health/smiling -can-trick-your-brain-happiness-boost-your-health -ncna822591.

TWSH.org. "What Is Domestic Violence?" The Women's Safe House. Accessed May 3, 2020. TWSH.org/community -education/what-is-dv/?.

White, Lesli. "What the Bible Really Says about Infidelity." Beliefnet. Accessed May 3, 2020. Beliefnet.com/love-family /relationships/affairs-and-divorce/what-the-bible-really -says-about-infidelity.aspx.

Whitley, Rob. "Religion and Mental Health: What Is the Link?" *Psychology Today.* December 18, 2017. PsychologyToday.com /us/blog/talking-about-men/201712/religion -and-mental-health-what -is-the-link.

INDEX

ACKNOWLEDGMENTS

To my loving family. Thank you for your love and support throughout the tireless hours of writing this book. I still remember the excitement on your faces when I shared with you all that I would be writing a new book! My heart melted knowing I always have your support and love. This book was written during the coronavirus pandemic, when we were all quarantined in our homes and forced to slow down and spend more time together. During the latter months of my writing you sacrificed some of your time with me to allow me to write, and we would make up for it through fun dates, dancing in the living room, and countless games of Uno. You all understand my passion to help families, and in return God is giving us so much love, laughter, and joy! Our family is the very foundation that I wrote about in this book. The best is yet to come as we continue to go where God sends us and impact who God desires us to impact.

ABOUT THE AUTHOR

PATRICE WEBB BUSH is the founder and CEO of It Takes 2 Marriage Coaching, which strengthens families through premarital and marital counseling, marriage retreats and workshops, and support groups and keynote speaking. With dual certifications in counseling and social work, she speaks from both academic and personal experience. The author of *Celebrate Our Love Couple's Journal: 120 Activities to Make Connecting Fun*, she has appeared on television and radio shows, keynoted major events, and hosted events across the country.